AL-RIDDAH AND THE MUSLIM CONQUEST OF ARABIA

AL-RIDDAH AND THE MUSLIM CONQUEST OF ARABIA

by

ELIAS SHOUFANI

UNIVERSITY OF TORONTO PRESS
THE ARAB INSTITUTE FOR RESEARCH AND PUBLISHING

First Published 1973 in Canada and the United States
by University of Toronto Press, Toronto and Buffalo
Reprinted in 2018

ISBN 0–8020–1915–3

ISBN 978-1-4875-8099-5 (paper)

Printed in Lebanon

TABLE OF CONTENTS

INTRODUCTION

The Problem of the Riddah

By the term Riddah, Muslim historiography denotes the "defection" of the tribes in Arabia from Islam after the death of the prophet Muḥammad; and by the term *Ḥurūb al-Riddah,* war of apostasy, it denotes the war which Abū Bakr, the first caliph, waged against the Arabs in the Arabian peninsula to bring them under the control of the Islamic state in Medina. The application by Muslim historians of these terms to movements in Arabia following the prophet's death emanated from their conviction that Muḥammad had converted most of Arabia to Islam during his lifetime and that the Arabs fell away from the religion after his death and, therefore, had to be fought and reconverted. This view of Muslim historians has been contested by modern students of Islamic history, especially in the West.

In view of the diversity of opinions with regard to the extent of Muḥammad's control over Arabia and the immediate relevance of this question to the understanding of the Riddah, I have attempted in the first chapter to examine this problem and to determine, on the basis of a re-examination of the sources, the extent of Muḥammad's success in his efforts to spread the domination of Islam over Arabia.

Other aspects of the problem of the Riddah to which students of early Islamic history have addressed themselves have been the question of the character and extent of that movement and its relation to the Arab conquest movement. The underlying assumption in traditional accounts concerning the Riddah is that it was a religious movement and that the wars of al-Riddah were separate from those of expansion, which are known as *futūḥ*. This assumption also has been contested by modern historians. In chapters III and IV, I have dealt with these two questions, seeking to clarify the issues involved.

Finally, much has been said about the Arab conquest movement's success in the territories of the Byzantine and Persian empires. I thought it only appropriate to devote chapter II to the constellation of forces which brought Abū Bakr to the seat of power and chapter V to the factors which contributed to his success in conquering Arabia.

Major Events During the Caliphate of Abu Bakr[1]

It has been commonly accepted that Muḥammad, the prophet of Islam, died on Rabi' I, 13, 11 A.H./June 8, 632 A.D., at the house of his beloved wife 'A'ishah, daughter of his closest associate and successor, the first caliph of Islam—Abū Bakr.[2] And, although a point of chronic dispute among Muslim sects, it has been generally accepted among students of Islamic history that the prophet did not leave any instructions for succession to his political position in the Muslim community of Medina.[3] Thus it was that the death of its spiritual and political leader confronted the young Muslim community with a dangerous crisis: a crisis which was caused by the rivalry among the various groups within that community for the succession to the prophet's political position. It is a well-

[1]The chronological arrangement of this survey is based mainly on Leone Caetani's *Chronographia Islamica*, Paris, 1912. An extensive list of references is given in this chronography to support Caetani's conclusions.

[2]Caetani, *Chro.*, I, 109; Sir William Muir, *The Caliphate, Its Rise, Decline and Fall*, revised edition by T.H. Weir, Edinburgh, 1924, p. 1; Bernard Lewis, *The Arabs in History*, 1958 (Grey Arrow Edition), p. 47.

[3]Caetani, *Chro.*, I, 109; Lewis, *op. cit.*, p. 50; C.H. Becker, "The Expansion of the Saracens," *The Cambridge Medieval History*, II, p. 332.

known episode in the annals of Islam that no sooner did Muḥammad die that the Anṣār, the Medinan Muslims, held a meeting to deliberate about a successor and proceeded to proclaim one of their members caliph. This was not acceptable to the Muhājirūn, the immigrants from Mecca, who held the view that they were more entitled to the position. Among the Muhājirūn, there was a faction of the prophet's kinsmen and their following who viewed themselves as the legitimate heirs to what "their man" had established. The frictions beween these three contending groups brought the community to the brink of fratricidal strife.[4]

The prevalent view among the historians of this early period of Islam is that the full crisis was averted only by a resolute act undertaken by three prominent members of the early companions of the prophet—Abū Bakr, Abū 'Ubaydah, and 'Umar. The success of their resolution was facilitated by the jealousies among the tribes of Medina.[5] This view is based on the Sunni tradition that the three companions, as it is told, rushed to the meeting-place of the Anṣār, put down the agitation, and carried away the assembled people to elect Abū Bakr caliph. This took place on the same day the prophet died.[6] On the following day, the proclamation of the new caliph was made public in the mosque where he delivered his traditionally well-known speech.[7] 'Ali, cousin and son-in-law of the prophet, however, refrained from giving his oath of allegiance, *bay'ah,* to the new caliph.[8]

Outside Medina, the death of the prophet, so the tradition asserts, caused profound commotion. In Mecca, in Hijāz, and in all Arabia for that matter, tribes were agitated, disorder

[4]Caetani, *Chro.*, I, 110; Lewis, *op. cit.*, p. 50-51; Muir, *op. cit.*, p. 2-3.

[5]Muir, *op. cit.*, p. 2-4; Caetani, *Chro.*, I, 110; Lewis, *op. cit.*, p. 51; see also H. Lammens, "Le triumverat Aboū Bakr, 'Omar, et Aboū 'Obaida," MUSJ 4 (1910), 113-114.

[6]Caetani, *Chro.*, I, 110; Lewis, 51.

[7]Caetani, *Chro.*, I, 110.

[8]Muir, 5.

burst in various parts of the peninsula, and many tribes detached themselves from Medina by refusing to pay the tax, or by following other prophets.[9] This movement of severing whatever ties the tribes of Arabia had with Medina is known in the Muslim tradition by the name of Riddah, apostasy.[10] The subjugation of this movement was the main task which occupied Abū Bakr throughout most of his caliphate of about two years.

The first task to be undertaken by the newly elected caliph, however, was to dispatch to its destination an expedition which was prepared by the prophet before his death. On his return from the last pilgrimage—Ḥijjat al-Wadāʿ, the prophet ordered his followers to prepare for a campaign to al-Balqā'—on the Syrian border. Muḥammad, however, died before the departure of the army and the expedition was suspended. Abū Bakr, reportedly, ordered that army to march on Syria, on the second day following his proclamation as caliph. In compliance with the prophet's word, the first caliph entrusted Usāmah b. Zayd b. Ḥārithah, son of a previously adopted son of the prophet, with the command of that campaign. Usāmah attacked southern Syria and, allegedly, returned with a large quantity of booty.[11]

After the departure of Usāmah and his army, the vast majority of the tribes in Arabia fell away from Medina. Only Mecca, Medina, and their surroundings remained loyal to Islam. The Muslim agents to the "apostatizing" tribes were forced to flee their posts and return hurriedly to Medina. Arabia revolted against Muslim Medina, and many tribes shifted position and followed rivals of Muḥammad who laid

[9]Caetani, *Chro.*, I, 111; Muir, 11.

[10]The technical Arabic term for apostasy is *irtidād.* However, the term *riddah* gained currency and replaced *irtidād*, and has been usually translated as apostasy or secession. See Lewis, *op. cit..*, 50; Henri Laoust, *Les schismes dans l'Islam*, Paris, 1965, 2 ff.

[11]Caetani, *Chro.*, I, 109 & 111; Muir, 9; M. de Goeje, *Mémoir sur la conquête de la Syrie*, Leiden, 1900, 17.

claim to prophethood.[12] In the face of these revolts, which erupted in various parts of the peninsula, Abū Bakr stood resolute and decisive in his refusal to negotiate new agreements with the "rebels"—other than those they had already concluded with the prophet. The first caliph, despite the counsel of his associates to the contrary, decided to force the apostatizing tribes to surrender. For this purpose the caliph prepared an expedition against the apostates, led it himself first, and later entrusted Khālid b. al-Walīd with its command.[13]

The first military action against the apostatizing tribes to the north-east of Medina was taken by Abū Bakr. There, the tribes of Ghaṭafān and Ṭayyi' allied themselves with Asad under the command of the latter's chief, Ṭalḥah b. Khuwaylid, in an attempt to defend themselves against Medina.[14] The main camp of these allied forces was at al-Buzākhah, a spring of water in the territory of Asad—but there were other smaller camps. In the second half of Jumādā II, 11 A.H./September 632, Abū Bakr clashed with and defeated one of the smaller camps at Dhū al-Qaṣṣah, notheast of Medina.[15] After this battle the rebels from Ghaṭafān fled and united with the main camp at al-Buzākhah, and Abū Bakr entrusted Khālid b. al-Walīd with the command of the army and dispatched him against the main camp. Khālid, before engaging in battle with the allies, succeeded in detaching Ṭayyi' from the alliance and having them join his forces against the remaining Asad and Ghaṭafān. With the help of Ṭayyi', Khālid fought and defeated the camp of al-Buzākhah and brought those tribes under the authority of Medina.[16] According to Caetani, the battle of al-Buzākhah took place in the month of

[12]Caetani, *Chro.*, I, 111; Muir, 11; Arnold Hottinger, *The Arabs*, University of California Press, 1963, 34.

[13]Caetani, *Chro.*, I, 111; Muir, 19.

[14]*E. I.*, articles "Tulaiḥah" by V. Vacca; "Taiy" by H.H. Braü; "Asad" by H. Kindermann; "Ghaṭafān" by J. W. Fück.

[15]Caetani, *Ibid.*

[16]Muir, 19-20; Caetani, *Ibid.*

Rajab-Sha'bān 11/October 632.[17]

From al-Buzākhah, Khālid advanced in the land of Tamīm, a large tribe—partly Christian and partly pagan—which inhabited the area between al-Yamāmah and the mouth of the Euphrates.[18] Among the Tamīm, a commotion that ended in fratricidal conflict was caused by the appearance, in the tribe, of the prophetess Sajāḥ.[19] When Khālid approached the land of Tamīm, the largest part of the tribe hastened to tender its submission to the Muslim army. Mālik b. Nuwayrah, chief of Yarbū', a branch of Tamīm, however, hesitated and stood aloof. Khālid, therefore, staged a surprise attack on Yarbū' in the camp of al-Buṭāḥ. Mālik was captured and put to death, apparently, on the orders of Khālid and despite the objection of many leaders in the Muslim army.[20]

To the east of Medina, in al-Yamāmah, and while Muḥammad was at the height of his power, a man known in the Muslim tradition by the contemptuous diminutive name of Musaylimah,[21] from Maslamah, rose to leadership among the powerful tribe of Banū Ḥanīfah—a section of Bakr b. Wā'il.[22]

Musaylimah laid claim to prophethood, challenging that of Muḥammad himself. Having subjugated Tamīm to the authority of Medina, Khālid moved towards al-Yamāmah and on the plain of 'Aqrabā' he encountered Musaylimah with his staunch supporters from Banū Ḥanīfah. The Muslims won a great victory in that battle, costly in human lives, which took place, according to Caetani in Rabī' I, 12 A.H./May-June 633.[23] After the victory, Khālid concluded a peace treaty with those from Banū Ḥanīfah who escaped the mass slaughter in what was to be known as the "Garden of Death," *Hadiqat*

[17]Caetani, *Ibid.*
[18]*E.I.*, "Tamīm" by G. Levy Della Vida; Muir, 23.
[19]*E.I.*, "Sadjāh" by V. Vacca; Muir, 24; Caetani, *Ibid.*
[20]Caetani, *Chro.*, I, 112; Muir, 24-26.
[21]*E.I.*, "Musailima" by Fr. Buhl; Muir, 27-28.
[22]*E.I.*, "Hanīfa b. Ludjaym" by W. Montgomery Watt.
[23]Caetani, *Chro.*, I, 121; Muir, 28-32.

al-mawt. Following their defeat, Banū Ḥanīfah sent a delegation to Medina to declare their complete surrender to the authority of the caliph of Islam.[24]

From al-Yamāmah, Khālid advanced with part of his army towards Baḥrayn, on the eastern coast of Arabia, to help al-ʻAlā' b. al-Ḥaḍramī, who was already engaged, on the orders of the caliph, in war with the rebels there. The rebels in Baḥrayn were in arms, under the command of one al-Ḥuṭam, and a scion of the Lakhmid dynasty from al-Hīrah by the name of al-Nuʻmān b. al-Mundhir al-Gharūr.[25] The revolt in Baḥrayn started after the death of al-Mundhir b. Sāwā al-ʻAbdī. Al-Mundhir was previously the agent of the Persians in Baḥrayn who accepted the suzerainty of Muḥammad and had received the above-mentioned al-ʻAlā' as a resident in his court in the capacity of agent from Medina.[26] Although al-Ḥuṭam was routed in a surprise attack by al-ʻAlā', the war went on a few more years in Baḥrayn before that area surrendered completely to Islam.[27] Khālid's role in the war in Baḥrayn is not clear in the sources, but while he was there, he received orders from the caliph to march and join the forces of the tribe of Bakr b. Wā'il in invading Persian territories in Iraq.[28]

While Khālid b. al-Walīd pursued his victorious career in central and eastern Arabia, other Muslim commanders, dispatched by Abū Bakr, were fighting other "apostates" elsewhere in Arabia.[29] To Yemen the caliph sent al-Muhājir b. Abī Umayyad to crush a movement against Islam which started during the prophet's lifetime. Headed by al-Aswad, who also laid claim to prophethood, this movement attracted a sizeable army of followers, which enabled him to wrest the

[24]Caetani, *Ibid.*
[25]Caetani, *Chro.*, I, 122.
[26]Muir, 33.
[27]Caetani, *Ibid.*
[28]Caetani, *Ibid.*
[29]Muir, 33.

rule over Ṣan'ā' from the Abnā'—the Persian ruling class in Yemen.[30] Al-Aswad's bad rule after having captured Ṣan'ā' caused strong resentment of him among the inhabitants and encouraged his rivals to conspire against him. With the help of his wife, the conspirators succeeded in entering his palace and murdering him in Rabī' I, 11 A.H./May-June 632.[31] After the assassination of al-Aswad, the Abnā' returned to Ṣan'ā' and reassumed their leadership. But, a new conflict between the Abnā' and the leaders of the Arab tribes in Yemen started. This conflict developed into a civil war, the result of which was the expulsion of the Persians from Ṣan'ā'.[32] In the wake of chaotic political conditions in Yemen, Abū Bakr dispatched al-Muhājir b. Abī 'Umayyah on an expedition aiming at the conquest of Yemen. Al-Muhājir succeeded in his mission: Qays b. Makshūḥ al-Murādī, leader of the Arab movement against the Persians, was defeated, captured, and sent to Medina. Yemen was pacified and made to recognize the caliph's authority.[33]

In south-eastern Arabia, 'Ikrimah b. Abī Jahl, commander of the Muslim army that was dispatched to quell the rebellion in 'Umān, defeated Laqīṭ b. Mālik—leader of the rebels—conquered and occupied Dabbā, capital of 'Umān, and proceeded to Mahrah. In Mahrah, 'Ikrimah defeated Shikhrīt, head of the rebels there, and subjugated that area.[34] From Mahrah, 'Ikrimah proceeded to join with al-Muhājir, who after pacifying Yemen went on to put down the rebels in Ḥaḍramawt. In Ḥaḍramawt, the injustice committed by the Muslim tax collectors caused a revolt against them there. Ḥaḍramawt, however, was conquered and brought under the

[30] *E.I.*, "al-Aswad al-'Ansi" by W. Montgomery Watt; "al-Abnā'" by K. N. Eettenstien.

[31] Caetani, *Chro.*, I, 113.

[32] Caetani, *Ibid.*, & 123.

[33] Caetani, *Ibid.*

[34] Caetani, *Chro.*, I, 122.

control of Medina.[35] With the conquest of Ḥaḍramawt, the whole peninsula became subject to the rule of the caliph in Medina.

While the Muslim armies were still fighting in south and south-eastern Arabia, Khālid b. al-Walīd, as has been pointed out above, was, on the invitation of the tribe of Bakr b. Wā'il, ordered by the caliph to invade Iraq. In the surroundings of al-Ḥīrah, capital of the Lakhmids, Khālid staged several successful raids on Arab-inhabited towns and forced the people of al-Ḥīrah itself to conclude a treaty with him. According to that treaty al-Ḥīrah was to pay an annual tribute to the Muslim state. At al-Ḥīrah, Khālid received the orders from the caliph to march to Syria and to join the Muslim armies there.[36]

Caetani held the view that Abū Bakr reached the decision to invade Syria only after his return from the *'Umrah*—smaller pilgrimage—in Rajab, 12 A.H./September 633.[37] On his return to Medina, the caliph dispatched three armies to Syria and ordered Khālid b. al-Walīd to march from Iraq and to join with the Muslims in Syria.[38] The conquest of Syria began. How the view held in this work differs from accepted views is discussed fully as the relation between the Riddah and the conquest movement.

[35]Caetani, *Ibid.*, 123.
[36]Caetani, *Ibid.*, 124.
[37]Caetani, *Ibid.*
[38]Caetani, *Ibid.*

1. MUHAMMAD'S CONTROL IN ARABIA

When the help of God and victory come, and thou seest men entering God's religion in throngs—then proclaim the praise of thy Lord and seek His forgiveness, for He turns again unto men.

—*Koran,* cx: i-3.

WHEREAS THIS VERSE OF THE KORAN TELLS OF "men entering God's religion in throngs," it does not support the thesis that Muslim tradition claims it supports: that virtually *all* the tribes of Arabia converted to Islam in the last two years of Muḥammad's lifetime. According to the tradition, the conversion to Islam was confirmed by deputations, *wufūd*, sent to Medina by each tribe. The year 9 A.H. is known traditionally as the Year of Deputations, *'ām al-wufūd*, because large numbers of tribal envoys converged on Medina that year to pay homage to Muḥammad and declare their tribes' allegiance to Islam.

The biographies of the prophet present us with long lists of the tribes that sent deputations to Medina.[1] But these sources

[1]Please see list of Bibliographical Abbreviations immediately preceding the Introduction. Sources referred to with great frequency will be abbreviated here as listed. Isḥāq, IV, 221 ff.; Aḥmad ibn Abī Ya'qūb al-Ya'qūbī (d. 897), *Tārīkh al-Yaqūbī*, II, 79; Sa'd, I/II, 38-86; Bal. *Ans.*, I, 530. A complete list of the deputations is found in Caetani's *Chronographia* (years 9 and 10) and his *Annali* for the same years.

are not clear about the obligations of the tribes towards Medina and from many reports we learn simply that a delegation from this or that tribe arrived in Medina, was presented with a gift from the prophet, and returned home. It seems, however, that for Muslim historians the arrival of a deputation to Medina signified the tribe's adoption of Islam and, consequently, its acceptance of the obligation to perform the prayer, *ṣalāt*, and to pay the tax, *zakāt*.

This view of classical Muslim historians has been contested by modern students of Islamic history, especially in the West. In the East, some conservative Muslim historians have accepted the classical view at face value while others have admitted its exaggeration. Examples follow of differing evaluations of Muḥammad's achievements—from representative works on the subject.

At the beginning of the century, for instance, Carl H. Becker, the German historian, in his well-known article about the Muslim conquest in *The Cambridge Medieval History* rejects the traditional view of Muḥammad's achievements and sums them up as follows:

> In reality Mahomet, at the time of his death, had by no means united Arabia, much less had he converted all the country to Islam. Not quite all of what today forms the Turkish province of Ḥijāz, that is the central portion of the west coast of Arabia with its corresponding back-country, was in reality politically joined with Medina and Mecca as a united power, and even this was held together more by interest than by religious brotherhood. The tribes of central Arabia, e.g., the Ghaṭafān, Bāhila, Tayyi', Asad, etc. were in a state of somewhat lax dependence on Mahomet and had probably also partially accepted the doctrine of Islam, whilst the Christian district to the north and in Yamāma, which had its own prophet, and in the south and east of the peninsula Mahomet either had no connexion whatever or had made

> treaties with single or isolated tribes, i.e., with a weak minority.[2]

In a generally similar fashion, in *Studi di Storia Orientali*, Leone Caetani divided the Arab tribes into four groups, after methodically and meticulously studying each tribe's relations with Muḥammad. The tribes in the vicinity of Mecca and Medina, the first group, submitted to Muḥammad and converted to Islam. The second group of tribes submitted politically to Muḥammad, and Islam made some progress among them; these were the tribes of Hawāzin, 'Amir, Ṭayyi', Sulaym, and possibly Khath'am. The third group was composed of the tribes who lived on the peripheries of the state of Medina; they submitted politically to Islam and were euphemistically called Muslims. The fourth group was made up of tribes who kept their independence from Medina, and among whom only a small minority sought the help of the prophet against adversaries; among these were Banū Ḥanīfah, 'Abd al-Qays, Azd 'Uman, and Haḍramawt.[3]

Contrary to the foregoing views, sceptical of the tradition, the Muslim scholar, M. Hamidullah, in his *Le Prophète de l'Islam*, champions the traditional view that Muḥammad established the state of Medina starting with a small area that was continually enlarged until it included all Arabia. Following the campaign to Tabūk, the whole peninsula, some areas in southern Iraq and Palestine were all under the control of the prophet. For Hamidullah, those areas were Islamized as well.[4] Other Eastern historians of Arabia admit that the tradition is not precise in its evaluation of the prophet's

[2]Becker, *op. cit.*, 334.

[3]Leone Caetani, *Studi di Storia Orientali* (Milano, 1911-1914), Vol. III, 346-349. See also Philip Hitti, *History of the Arabs* (London, 1964), 141; Lewis, *op. cit.*, 47.

[4]Muhammad Hamidullah, *Le Prophète de l'Islam* (Paris, 1959), Vol. I, 433-434. See also M.H. Haykal, *Hayāt Muḥammad*, 480; Shukrī Faysal, *Harakāt al-Fatḥ al-Islāmī*, 1; M. al-Khuḍarī, *Tārīkh al-Umam al-Islāmīyah*, 143.

achievements in the Arabian peninsula. A. A. Dūrī, for example, acknowledges that some tribes aligned themselves with Medina only politically, others regarded the tax as humiliating and grudgingly submitted to Medina, and others aligned themselves neither politically nor religiously with Islam.[5] The same views as Dūrī's are held by another Arab historian of this early period of Islam, 'Abd al-Mun'im Mājid.[6]

With regard to the problem of the extent to which Muḥammad controlled Arabia, the views of M. Watt, author of the most up-to-date and comprehensive biography of the prophet, are of special importance because they are the result of a receptive but judicial approach to the sources. In Watt's words, Muḥammad's achievements were as follows:

> Finally, we have to ask to what extent the tribes were in at least political alliance with Muḥammad. Those in the neighborhood of Medina and Mecca were all firmly united to him. So also were those of the center and along the route to 'Irāq, but there were some exceptions. In the Yemen and the rest of the South-West there were numerous groups in alliance, but they may not have been more than half the population. In the South-East the proportion was probably less. Along the route to Syria there had been little success in detaching tribes from the Byzantine emperor.
>
> Thus Muḥammad had not altogether succeeded in unifying Arabia, but he had done more than sceptical European scholars have allowed. Moreover, his personal influence doubtless gave him power and authority beyond that conferred by formal agreements, for example in the affairs of tribes which were in alliance with him on equal

[5] 'Abd al-'Azīz al-Dūrī, *Muqaddima fi tārīkh ṣadr al-Islam* (Beirut, 1960), 42-43.

[6] 'Abd al-Mun'im Mājid, *al-Tārīkh al-siyāsī lī-al-dawlah al-Arabīyah* (Cairo, 1956-67), 144-145.

> footing. There were certainly gaps but except in the North-West they were inconsiderable. The framework of unity had been built. A political system with strong foundations had been erected, into which the tribes could be brought. Many had come in, others could be easily added.

For the purpose of discussion, it is most practicable to divide Arabia into geographical regions and examine the extent of Muḥammad's control in each. In the course of the discussion, consideration will be given to the political aspects of relations between Muḥammad and the tribes and special attention devoted to those tribes which supposedly defected immediately following Muḥammad's death. This will help us to carry the discussion through the caliphate of Abū Bakr, under whose rule the conquest of Arabia took place. We shall consider the regions of Arabia in this order: the Ḥijāz, Najd, the coastal areas, and the north.

THE ḤIJAZ

Mecca, Medina, and Ṭā'if were the three main cities in the Ḥijāz. The *Hijrah*, or emigration to Medina from Mecca in 622 A.D., gave Muḥammad a new base from which to pursue his struggle to spread the hegemony of Islam over Arabia. A decade of active preaching in his native city with little success made it clear to Muḥammad that the expansion of his movement was being blocked by the powerful opposition in Mecca and that a new strategy must be adopted if any further success were to be achieved. It became obvious that the Meccans would have to be fought and defeated before they would submit to Islam. Such an active strategy against Mecca would necessitate that Muḥammad establish uncontested leadership at headquarters outside Mecca and conclude agreements with the tribes inhabiting the areas astride the Meccan trade routes. After the *Hijrah*, Muḥammad lost no time in implementing this strategy.

On his arrival in Medina, the prophet by no means became the uncontested leader of the town. The Constitution of Medina provided that Muḥammad serve as chief of the *Muhājirūn*, the immigrants, and that these be considered a clan with equal privileges and responsibilities as the other clans inhabiting the town. The only extra privilege he had was that disputes among the various clans would be referred to him for arbitration.[8] His freedom of action against the Meccans, however, was limited by the fact that the Medinans had pledged to protect him against enemies but had not undertaken any obligation to fight offensive battles on his behalf.[9] Therefore, Muḥammad had to lure the Medinans subtly into open warfare with the Meccans. And his tactics caused much bitter friction inside Medina between his devout followers and his opponents, who are usually referred to by the Muslim tradition as the *Munāfiqūn*, the Hypocrites.[10] But the most problematic of Muḥammad's tests was his struggle against the Meccans—in the course and as a result of which he overcame the other difficulties.

* * *

The final capitulation of Mecca to Muḥammad was achieved in four discernible stages. The first was characterized by hit and run guerrilla-like ambushes of Meccan trade caravans; the second contained full-scale battles; the third was an armistice of sorts which culminated in a peace agreement; the short fourth stage is characterized by diplomatic maneuvres which led to the Meccan capitulation.[11]

[7]Montgomery Watt, *Muḥammad at Medina* (Oxford U.P., London, 1956), 149. Hereafter, when a reference is simply to "Watt"—it is to this work.

[8]Watt, 228-229.

[9]Watt, 231.

[10]About the internal politics of Medina, cf. Watt, Ch. V.

[11]About the struggle between Muḥammad and the Meccans, cf. Watt, Chapters I, II, & III.

Stage One

Muḥammad and his early companions were all Meccans familiar with the workings of that mercantile society. Mecca's life-line was its trade and the prophet was fully aware that by striking at this sensitive conduit he could bring the Meccans to their knees. Thus, we note that all the early campaigns, *maghāzi*, of Muḥammad up to the battle of Badr (2 A.H.) were directed against the caravans. There is some disagreement in the sources as to the number, order, and dates of the early campaigns, but they agree generally that all these campaigns attempted to intercept Meccan caravans without much success.[12] The prophet and his companions reaped little booty but much trouble from ambushing some Meccans at Nakhlah on their way back from Ṭā'if during a sacred month.[13]

The salient feature of these early razzias, *maghāzi*, are: a relatively small number of participants, the absence of any native Medinans, the failure of the razzias to yield any substantive material gains. The relative fruitlessness of the razzias is not surprising considering the small number of staunch early Muhājirūn, the nature of the Anṣār pledge to Muḥammad, and the skillful Meccan management of their trade caravans. In case after case, the sources tell of well-manned caravans able to defend themselves and of well-led ones that had eluded the Muslims and passed on safely.[14] Some of these little campaigns, however, yielded significant results in that Muḥammad succeeded in concluding non-aggression pacts with several of the tribes on the trade route, thus securing a less hostile environment for his activities.[15]

[12]Isḥāq, I, 591-601; Wāqidī, I, 9-13; Bal. *Ans.*, I, 287.

[13]The similarity of stories on Nakhlah in the sources is noteworthy; see Isḥāq, I, 601-605; Wāqīdī, I, 13-18.

[14]Isḥāq, I, 591-595; Wāqidī, I, 9-13; Bal. *Ans.*, I, 287.

[15]Isḥāq, I, 591 & 595 & 599; Wāqidī, I, 9 & 11; Bal. *Ans.*, I, 287.

Stage Two

The second phase of Muḥammad's struggle with the Meccans started with the battle of Badr in the month of Ramadān of the year 2 A.H. (March 624 A.D.). Muḥammad with a large number of his followers including Anṣār had stepped up his activity by trying to intercept a large caravan on its way back from Syria.[16] The Meccans, in turn, had become disturbed about the future of their trade and had decided to put an end to the irksome presence of Muḥammad. Under the leadership of the astute Abū Sufyān, the caravan eluded Muḥammad this time also. But the Meccans came in arms to rescue their property in response to Abū Sufyān's call for help and, seeing the small band of Muslims, felt the moment opportune for teaching the Muslims a lesson and thus preserving their own prestige among the Arab tribes.[17] The two sides lined up for the battle, and the Muslims won a decisive victory over the Meccans, who, according to traditional sources, were threefold as many.

The Muslims saw the hand of God behind this victory. In the *Koran* as well as in the tradition, the story of Gabriel at the head of an army of angels fighting on the Muslim side is ubiquitous.[18] Only a small portion of the Medinans had joined Muḥammad in this campaign. However, without their presence this battle could not have been conceived, for though they were few they were the bulk of his army. Many of those who later became devout followers of the prophet had stayed behind in Medina.[19] According to traditional sources, the non-participants gave the excuse that no fighting had been anticipated; it was, they had thought, simply a matter of ambushing the caravan.[20] These same sources, however,

[16]Isḥāq, I, 615; Wāqidī, I, 49; Bal. *Ans.*, I, 290.
[17]Isḥāq, I, 619; Wāqidī, I, 44; Bal. *Ans.*, I, 291.
[18]See Wāqidī, I, 56-57.
[19]Isḥāq, I, 607; Wāqidī, I, 21; Bal. *Ans.*, I, 288.
[20]*Ibid.*

assert that before the battle the prophet had doubted the willingness of those Anṣār who were present to join him against the Meccans. The Anṣār, we are told, assured the prophet that they would not desert him at this point.[21] Having been induced to join Muḥammad in the booty-promising campaign when no serious fighting was foreseen,[22] these Anṣār found themselves in the difficult position of having to make a momentous decision either to fight and incur Meccan animosity or withdraw from the scene of the battle and swallow their pride. They opted for the former.

The Anṣār were thus drawn irrevocably and probably inadvertantly into the center of conflict. Many Meccans were killed or captured and their tribe, Quraysh, was under the customary obligation of avenging their blood. The Medinans could not at this point wash their hands of their responsibility *vis à vis* the Meccans, and in the eyes of the Meccans they had become full-fledged party to the conflict. The Medinans, by cooperating in Muḥammad's agressive action, had rendered null and void their pledge to Muḥammad of merely defensive support. The acts of the few at Badr had become, according to Arab customary law, the collective responsibility of the whole Medinan community. The whole of Medina at the same time became the target of Meccan vengeance, and the only option left open for Medina was to fight and defend itself. As for Muḥammad, encouraged by his victory at Badr, he turned to consolidate his position in Medina in preparation for the second round with the Meccans, which was sure to be soon.

Having suffered a humiliating defeat at Badr and seeing no end to the menacing of their caravans, the Meccans, immediately on their return home, began the task of harnessing all their resources to redress their grievance and retrieve their prestige. A military expedition against Medina, financed by

[21]Isḥāq, I, 615; Wāqidī, I, 49.
[22]Ṭab., I, 1285.

the profits from the rescued caravan of Badr, was soon being readied.[23] In March, 625 A.D., a year after the debacle at Badr, the expedition set out from Mecca and a few days later arrived north of Medina and camped near Mount Uḥud. At Uḥud, the Meccans carried the day: the Muslims were routed, several of their leaders were killed, and the prophet himself was seriously wounded. The Quraysh thus avenged the blood of those who fell at Badr, proved their prowess, and redeemed their name among the Arab tribes.

In the battle of Uḥud, some Medinans had even fought on the Meccan side[24] and at least a third of the eligible men remained in the town and refused to engage in battle with the invading army.[25] This might well have been why the Meccan leadership counselled against invading the town and pushing their chances too far.[26] Yet, despite their winning this round, the Meccans were still far from putting a damper on Muḥammad's activity, because they had not touched his base of operations. On the contrary, after Uḥud, he intensified his efforts to draw more tribes of the area surrounding Mecca and Medina to his side.

Simultaneously, the Meccans were actively engaged in forming a confederacy—consisting of themselves, several powerful nomadic tribes, and a few Jewish tribes—this time, in preparation for the invasion of Medina. The confederates, reportedly, were ten thousand strong.[27] Their avowed aim was to do away with Muḥammad and his movement once and for all. The invasion took place in March, 627 A.D.

This time, however, Muḥammad, having learned his lesson from Uḥud, adopted a defensive strategy. He decided to stay inside the town and dig a trench around it—hence, the name of the battle, *al-Khandaq*. The confederates laid siege to the

[23]Isḥāq, II, 60; Wāqidī, I, 199-200; Bal. *Ans.*, I, 312.
[24]Wāqidī, I, 205; Bal. *Ans.*, I, 313.
[25]Isḥāq, II, 64; Wāqidī, I, 219; Bal. *Ans.*, I, 314.
[26]Wāqidī, I, 299.
[27]Isḥāq, II, 219.

town. The trench hindered the storming of Medina by the superior, invading cavalry. In addition to this stratagem, Muḥammad had resorted to sowing dissention among the heterogeneous confederates. He had bribed the leader of Ghaṭafān with the offer of a third of Medina's date-harvest if he would withdraw from the confederacy. He did.[28] Muḥammad also planted mistrust between the Jewish tribe of Qurayẓah and the rest of the confederacy.[29] The siege continued for two weeks, but finally broke up in discord among the allies; their costly campaign ended a fiasco. The Meccan failure at al-Khandaq marked the beginning of a new era of rising fortune for Muḥammad. From this point on, the Meccans were on the defensive and retreat.

Stage Three

This stage is of about three years duration and is distinguished by the relatively peaceful coexistence between the warring parties of the Ḥijāz, during which the path for Meccan surrender to Islam was paved. A milestone reached during this period of quiet Muslim-Meccan contention was a peace treaty concluded between the two parties at al-Ḥudaybiyeh in March of 628 A.D., a year after the battle of al-Khandaq.

Muḥammad had called upon his followers in Medina and upon some friendly tribes in that vicinity to march to Mecca in order to perform the '*Umrah*, or lesser pilgrimage. Many Medinans responded, but a few tribes, fearing renewed conflict with the Meccans, had abstained from going with the Muslims.[30] When the Muslims approached the sanctuary, the Meccans vowed not to allow them to enter the city by force.[31] The Muslims, for their part, assured the Meccans

[28]Isḥāq, II, 223; Wāqidī, II, 477; Abū 'Ubayd al-Qāsim ibn Sallām (770-837), *Kitāb al-amwāl al-Kharāj* (Cairo, 1934).

[29]Wāqidī, II, 480 ff.; Bal. *Ans.*, I, 345; Shaybānī, *Siyar*, I, 122.

[30]Isḥāq, II, 308; Wāqidī, II, 574.

[31]Isḥāq, II, 309; Wāqidī, II, 597; Ṭab., I, 1531; Bal. *Ans.*, I, 349.

that they came in peace to perform their religious rites and intended to depart as they had come. Anticipating that such an episode would be humiliating and detrimental to their prestige among the Arabs, the Meccans were prepared to do everything within their power, including fight, to prevent the Muslims from entering. The course of the ensuing events in this expedition indicates clearly that both sides wanted to avoid fighting so long as a face-saving solution for each could be found. Peace-makers went back and forth between them until a treaty acceptable to both was ratified.

According to that treaty, known as *al-Ḥudaybiyah*, the Muslims were to postpone the performance of the *'umrah* until the following year when the Meccans would evacuate the city for three days to allow the Muslims to conduct their religious rites freely. Other provisions of the treaty stipulated the abandonment of hostilities for ten years; freedom of other groups or individuals to enter into alliances with whichever side they favored; the extradition of any Meccan who joined the Muslims without the consent of his protector.[32]

In the light of Muḥammad's long-term policy, the treaty was a diplomatic victory. It served the prophet's strategy of taking Mecca without bloodshed and of making it the pivotal point for the propagation of Islam. By signing the treaty, Muḥammad established the right of the Muslims to the sanctuary on equal footing with the non-Muslims. Also, on the political front, he had become, by acknowledgement of the Meccans themselves, a peer of equal stature in the Ḥijāz. Furthermore, the treaty strengthened his position among his followers. Whereas the terms of the treaty, which to many of Muḥammad's followers seemed disadvantageous to Muslims, had caused widespread if temporary disappointment and bitterness among them—Muḥammad was able to turn the emotional tide to advantage. At this critical moment the prophet put his followers to test and procured their oath of

[32]Isḥāq, II, 317-318; Wāqidī, II, 611-612.

allegiance; this was the Pledge of Good Pleasure, *Bay'at al-Riḍwān.*[33]

Stage Four

In the final stage of Muḥammad's struggle against Mecca, his efforts were crowned by the surrender of the Meccans. They had violated the peace treaty by helping their allies, Banū Bakr, against Banū Khuzā'ah, the allies of Muḥammad. The two feuding tribes had been hostile towards each other for a long time before the advent of Islam. Each had seized the opportunity of the Ḥudaybiyah to align itself with one of the two contending parties.[34] The Meccans foresaw trouble with Muḥammad and delegated Abū Sufyān to renew the treaty.[35] Muḥammad, however, had other plans. By then, two years after the peace treaty, Muḥammad's power had grown to such an extent that the Meccans were no longer a match for him. It was time to march on Mecca and sieze it. The moment was opportune; his allies called upon him to come to their aid, and he did. Mecca capitulated almost without resistance.

After eight years of resistance, the Meccan aristocracy had realized the futility of its struggle with Muḥammad, and Mecca submitted to the prophet of Islam. Meccan leadership had failed to organize itself and to unite its ranks against the enemy in Medina. The social structure of the town of Mecca, its internal politics, and jealousies among the leading contenders for prominence in that town rendered it impossible for anyone of that group to assume leadership over the different Meccan clans.[36] In this respect, the situation in Mecca, at this juncture of its history, resembled to a great extent that of

[33]Isḥāq, II, 315; Wāqidī, II, 602-603; Abū 'Ubayd, *Amwāl*, 157.

[34]Isḥāq, II, 389; Wāqidī, II, 780; Ṭab., I, 1619; Bal. *Ans.*, I, 353; Bayhaqī, *Sunan*, IX, 120.

[35]Isḥāq, II, 395-397; Wāqidī, II, 791; Bal. *Ans.*, I, 355.

[36]Cf. Watt, 55-65.

Medina on the eve of its appeal to Muḥammad to move there and assume leadership over it. During the eight years of struggle against Muḥammad, the Meccans were not able to produce the new type of leadership they needed in order to deal successfully with the ever-growing threat to their trade, religion, social structure, and to their position among the Arabs. No one from among the Meccans had the power, prestige, and statesmanship to equal Muḥammad both as religious and political head. In the Ḥijāz, Muḥammad alone wielded enough power and had enough influence to set forth the claim for leadership of that area. In the course of achieving his goal, Muḥammad had fought and successfully overcome the Meccans, proving himself worthy of his claim. Frustration in the Meccan camp, on the other hand, and the ever-increasing efficacy of Muḥammad's retinue convinced several of the prominent leaders in Mecca that it would be more advantageous to them if they joined the Muslim camp.

Dissention with regard to the question of Muḥammad appeared as early as Badr among the leaders of the rival clans in Mecca. At Badr some leaders counselled against confrontation with the Muslims as long as the caravan seemed secure. Some tribes returned home once they learned that the caravan had eluded the Muslims and was safely on its way to Mecca.[37] At Uḥud, again, the Meccans would not drive their campaign to its victorious end: to put an end to the enemy in Medina. Likewise, the battle of al-Khandaq, divided counsel among the Meccans and betrayal by their allies had brought that expensive campaign to nothing and, indeed, had been detrimental to the Meccan cause. Disgusted with his allies and indignant about the lack of cohesion in the Meccan camp, Abū Sufyān, the prominent leader of the clan of Umayyah and reported commander of the confederacy that had laid siege on Medina, had decided to withdraw and return home. It was probably at this point—after the confederate fiasco

[37]Isḥāq, I, 619, 622-624; Wāqidi, I, 34-37, 63-65, 200.

and complete failure to achieve its declared aim of destroying Muhammad and of putting an end to his movement—that Abū Sufyān realized the futility of continuous conflicts with the Muslims, contemplated a negotiated peace with Muḥammad, and embarked on secret contacts with him in an effort to bring about a peaceful capitulation of Mecca to the prophet of Islam.

Without the supposition that there was a secret agreement between Muḥammad and Abū Sufyān's group, the events following al-Khandaq would be virtually inexplicable. First of all, it is hard to imagine the Muslims undertaking a pilgrimage to the heart of their enemy's territory only a short period after al-Khandaq without their first having secured the favorable attitude of a considerable portion of the inhabitants of Mecca.

The traditional sources tend to minimize the role played by those Meccans who helped to bring about the peaceful surrender of Mecca to Muḥammad—especially that of Abū Sufyān, head of the influential Umayyad clan. At the same time, the role of al-Abbās, forefather of the dynasty under which these source-works were written, is magnified. Despite the tendencious reports of the sources, they do not entirely obscure the decisive part Abū Sufyān had in the capitulation of Mecca.

Were there not some sort of agreement between Muḥammad and Abū Sufyān, how could the latter's absence from all negotiations at al-Ḥudaybiyah be explained? or the subsequent marriage of his daughter to Muḥammad? or the fact that he was the peace-maker when that treaty was broken about two years later? Abū Sufyān was in Mecca at the time of al-Ḥudaybiyah and did not participate in the negotiations; and 'Uthmān, who was sent by Muḥammad to negotiate with the Meccans for the Muslim's peaceful entry to the sanctuary, was a lodger at Abū Sufyān's house.[38] 'Uthmān, an Umay-

[38]Wāqidī, 600-601, Sa'd, II/I, 70; Athīr, II, 203; Nuwayrī, XVII, 226.

yad, was chosen to negotiate with the Meccans because of his connections with that prestigious clan. His clan protected him and abstained from hostilities against the Muslims.[39] Moreover, the prophet married the daughter of Abū Sufyān, Umm Ḥabībah, shortly after the peace treaty of al-Ḥudaybiyah.[40] And when the treaty was broken, Abū Sufyān was the mediator between the Meccans and the Muslims.[41] He is reported to have gone to Medina to negotiate a re-enactment of the peace treaty and to have met with Muḥammad at Marr al-Zahrān and to have become a Muslim before the army of Muḥammad entered Mecca. And the prophet honored the old enemy by declaring his house an asylum, *jiwār*.[42] Abū Sufyān entered Mecca with Muḥammad and the Muslim army as a highly esteemed ally and not as a humble, defeated enemy. In this manner, he saved the town from plunder and bloodshed[43] and diverted the Muslim arms against the Hawāzin, a strong tribe hostile to both Islam and Quraysh, in the area surrounding Ṭā'if.[44] It is highly unlikely that all these things involving Abū Sufyān happened coincidentally.

The prophet was appreciative of the services of Abū Sufyān and his party. After the capitulation of Mecca, the prominent leaders of Quraysh were treated with great respect by Muḥammad. The *jiwār* of Abū Sufyān was honored by the Muslims and the inhabitants of Mecca were not molested. Having succeeded in bringing the Meccans to the fold of Islam, the

[39]Wāqidī, *loc. cit.*

[40]Bal. *Ans.*, I, 438; Ṭab., I, 1772; Dhahabī, *'Ibar*, I, 8.

[41]Wāqidī, 792; Sa'd, II/I, 97; Ṭab., I, 1623; Bal. *Ans.*, I, 255; Bayhaqī, *Sunan*, IX, 120; Ḥalabī, III, 8.

[42]Wāqidī, 818, Sa'd, II/I, 98; Bal. *Ans.*, I, 335; Bayhaqī, *Sunan*, IX, 118; Nuwayrī, XVII, 302; Ḥalabī, III, 25; also see *E. I.*, article "Djiwār" by J. Lecerf.

[43]Wāqidī, 822 ff.; Bal. *Ans.*, I, 355; Bayhaqī, *Sunan*, IX, 121; Ḥalabī, III, 25.

[44]Wāqidī, 816; Ḥalabī, III, 19.

prophet was so anxious to please them that he aroused the indignation of the early Muhājirūn and the Anṣār.[45] The leaders of Quraysh were given generous gifts by the prophet from the booty won in the battle of Ḥunayn against the Hawāzin.[46] In the later years of Muḥammad's life, the majority of the governors, *'ummāl*, were drawn from the Meccan aristocrats.[47]

Mecca "the sanctuary" and Quraysh "the laqāḥ" (i.e., foremost tribe) were great assets to Muḥammad, just as Islam was to the Meccans. The *fatḥ*, conquest of Mecca, enhanced the Muslims' position in Arabia,[48] and it proved to be just as beneficial to the Meccans. By joining the Muslim camp, the skillful Qurayshites dominated the affairs of the Muslim community in a short time. Muḥammad knew how to employ Meccan skill and talent in the service of his movement; and they, in turn, soon learned how to exploit that movement outwards. He, a religious leader first and foremost, and they, a mercantile society, had the common interest of expansion, and they joined their energies to achieve it.

Right after the surrender of Mecca and probably on the initiative of the Meccans,[49] Muḥammad attacked the third and last center of power in the Ḥijāz.[50] The newly converted Meccans participated in the campaign against Ṭā'if and its surroundings, contributed much to its success, and profited from victory over Hawāzin.[51] The battle of Ḥunayn, against

[45]Wāqidī, 956 ff.; Sa'd, II/I, 111; Ibn Qutaybah, *Ma'ārif*, 163; Nuwayrī, XVII, 347.

[46]Wāqidī, 944-947; al-Suhaylī, *al-Rawḍ al-Unuf*, II, 308; al-Rāzī, *Tafsīr*, XVI, 111 (K. IX: 60); Ḥalabī, III, 85.

[47]Ibn Habīb, 126; Bal. *Ans.*, I, 529-530; al-Maqrīzī, Asbāb, 32-34; *E.I.*, article "'Amil" by A. A. Dūrī.

[48]Mas'ūdī, *Tanbīh*, 329; Watt, 65.

[49]Wāqidī, 816; Ḥalabī, III, 19.

[50]Watt, 70-73.

[51]Wāqidī, 890, 910, 929, 944ff.; Sa'd, II/I, 111; Mas'ūdī, *Tanbīh*, 234; Rāzī, *Tafsīr*, XVI, 111 (K. X:60).

the powerful Hawāzin, was the first cooperative and successful achievement of Muḥammad and his new Meccan allies; it signaled the beginning of the Arab conquest.

With the three main towns in the Ḥijāz lined up behind Muḥammad, the nomadic tribes around these centers lost their freedom and ability to maneuver. They were lurking to see the result of the struggle between Muḥammad and Mecca; and when Mecca surrendered, they followed suit.[52] "If I leave you, all the Arabs will leave you and neither horned nor unhorned goat will hurt thereafter," Abū Sufyān is reported to have said in jest to the prophet.[53] The bedouins of the Ḥijāz joined the Muslim state and identified their interest with that of the state to the degree that a separate history has not been recorded for them.[54] These tribes remained faithful to Abū Bakr and supplied contingents to the Muslim army that conquered the rest of Arabia.[55]

As the leader of all the Ḥijāz, Muḥammad wielded more power than anyone else in Arabia at that time. His power and position induced many troubled chiefs of tribes to seek his help and support against local, rival chiefs.[56] But the winning of the Meccans to his side and, consequently, the surrender of the Ḥijāz were Muḥammad's greatest political achievements. The conquest of the rest of Arabia and of the Fertile Crescent was, in the main, the work of Meccans. They led the Arabs to victory over the Byzantines and the Persians.

* * *

[52]Isḥāq, 985; Mas'ūdi, *Tanbīh*, 239; Athīr, II, 226; Diyārbakrī, II, 192; Wellhausen, *Tārikh*, 20; Demombynes, *Mahomet*, Paris, 1967, 208.

[53]Suhayli, II, 276; Ibn Hajar, *Iṣābah*, II, 172.

[54]Becker, *op. cit.*, 334; Lewis, 51; Watt, 87; Mājid, I, 144-145.

[55]Watt, *loc. cit.*

[56]Wellhausen, *Skizzen*, VI, 7.

NAJD

In the area to the east of Medina there were several groups of tribes, the most important of which was Banū Ḥanīfah. To the northeast there were groups of Ghaṭafān, Ṭayyi', and Asad. And further away, Tamīm.

1) *Banū Hanīfah*

Muḥammad never did control Banū Ḥanīfah during his lifetime. This tribe with its center in Yamāmah was by far the strongest and most important in the area. Around the time of Muḥammad, Hawdhah b. 'Ali was the chief of this tribe and the local agent of the Persians in Yamāmah. Hawdhah, like many other Arab chiefs, carried the title *malik*,[57] literally "king", a title which apparently was used by the Arabs to designate those chiefs who were appointed the Persians or the Byzantines in the buffer princedoms these empires maintained at their borders. According to a poem by A'shā, Hawdhah was known as Dhū al-Tāj, the crowned,[58] and was in charge of the yearly, royal caravan, the *latīmah*, from Persia to Yemen.[59]

The sources speak of negotiations between Muḥammad and Hawdhah. The latter is mentioned among the six "kings" to whom Muḥammad wrote letters calling them to adopt Islam.[60] But the sources are not agreed on a date for this correspondence. Some give the year 6, others the year 7, and some refrain from giving any specific date. The year 6 as

[57]al-Mubarrad, III, 23; Bal. *Ans.*, I, 531; Athīr, II, 215; Ibn 'Abd Rabbih, II, 243-244; Diyārbakrī, II, 240.

[58]al-Mubarrad, III, 23; Ibn 'Abd Rabbih, II, 244; Diyārbakri, II, 240.

[59]Ibn 'Abd Rabbih, II, 243.

[60]Ibn Ḥabīb, 76; Sa'd, I/II, 18; Ṭab., I, 1559, 1561; Balādhurī, *Ans.*, I, 531; Bal. *Fut.*, 105; Diyārbakrī, II, 39, 182; about these letters, cf. M. Hamidullah, *Corpus des Traités et Lettres Diplomatiques de l'Islam, Documents sur la Diplomatie Musulmane, Majmū'at al-wathā'iq al-siyāsīyah li-al-'Ahd al-Nabawī.*

the date of Muḥammad's dispatching of the letters seems to originate with Wāqidī, while Ibn Isḥāq puts it between the Ḥudaybiyah, year 6, and the prophet's death, year 11. Those who give the year 7 seem to have made the calculation that the correspondence took place after Ḥudaybiyah and before the death of Hawdhah in the year 8.[61] None of the sources, however, puts it before Ḥudaybiyah, so we can assume that it took place shortly after the peace treaty with the Meccans. This assumption is quite reasonable and is compatible with Muḥammad's policy. Once he had secured peaceful co-existence with the Meccans, he turned to other parts of Arabia and tried to bring them under control.

Hawdhah's response to Muḥammad's feeler was anything but satisfactory. The reports on Hawdhah's stipulations and promises differ from one source to another, but all the sources agree on Muḥammad's rejection of whatever Hawdhah's stipulations were. According to one version, Hawdhah had stipulated that he share with Muḥammad the rule over Arabia,[62] while according to another he asked Muḥammad to appoint him as his successor.[63] The former, however, seems more plausible because of Hawdhah's advanced age.

The second clause in Hawdhah's reply is quite interesting and might shed some light on the nature of Muḥammad's letter to him. The sources are vague as regards the content of that letter. The majority among them do not say much and satisfy themselves with the general statement that he called Banū Ḥanīfah to adopt Islam.[64] In comparison with other letters reproduced in the sources in which Muḥammad is specific about the obligations of the addressee,[65] this one to Hawdhah seems to have been altered, probably intentionally,

[61] Sa'd, I/II, 15, 18; Bal. *Fut.*, 105 & *Ans.*, I, 531; Ṭab., I, 1559, 1560; Athīr, II, 215; Diyārbakrī, II, 182, 183.

[62] Sa'd, I/II, 18; Ibn Sayyid al-Nās, II, 269; Diyārbakrī, II, 40, 183.

[63] Bal. *Fut.*, I, 105; Athīr, II, 215.

[64] Sa'd, I/II, 18; Bal. *Fut.*, I, 105; Athīr, II, 215.

[65] Cf., for example, the letters in Ibn Sa'd, I/II, 19 ff.

to blacken Banū Ḥanīfah. Nevertheless, two different versions of the second clause in Hawdhah's reply exist in the sources. Those which originated in Wāqidī's works give a simple version: if Muḥammad were to meet the demands of Hawdhah, Hawdhah would follow him.[66] Balādhurī, however, gives the following: "If [Muḥammad] appoints [Hawdhah] as his successor, he [Hawdhah] will adopt Islam, march to him [Muḥammad] and help him," *naṣarahu*.[67] Ibn al-Athīr agrees with Balādhurī but adds: "Otherwise, he [Hawdhah] would fight him" (*qaṣada ḥarbahu*).[68] If we accept Ibn al-Athīr's version, we are confronted with an either-or kind of answer. This would indicate that Hawdhah had become concerned about the situation in the Ḥijāz and, probably, felt threatened by Muḥammad's rising power. If, on the other hand, we accept Balādhurī's version, we can assume that Muḥammad was seeking to establish an alliance, *munāṣarah*,[69] with Hawdhah, and the latter was presenting his terms for such an alliance. This confirms the conclusions arrived at by some modern biographers of Muḥammad regarding his relations with the distant and powerful tribes of Arabia.[70] Wāqidī's version seems to be influenced by religious motivation.

Balādhurī's account furnishes us with an answer to another problem, namely, that of the deputation from Banū Hanīfah to Medina. It has been suggested that the deputation came to Muḥammad of its own accord and only after the death of Hawdhah.[71] According to Balādhurī, the deputation came right after receiving the letter of Muḥammad.[72] This implies that Hawdhah was still alive. Ibn al-Athīr is even more

[66]Sa'd, I/II, 18, Ibn Sayyid al-Nās, II, 269.
[67]Bal. *Fut.*, I, 105.
[68]Athīr, II, 215.
[69]Cf. Emile Tyan, *Institutions du Droit Public Musulman*, I, 40-42.
[70]Watt, 144.
[71]Caetani, *Chro.*, I, 120; Watt, 134.
[72]Bal. *Fut.*, I, 105.

specific; he asserts that Hawdhah sent the deputation.[73]

Most of the traditional sources mention Musaylimah as a member of Banū Ḥanīfah's deputation.[74] Ibn al-Athīr, however, does not.[75] Balādhurī includes him and ascribes to him demands which were the same as those of Hawdhah.[76] Under these circumstances, it is hard to accept the assumption that Musaylimah was not a member of the deputation.[77] It is as difficult to accept the view that the whole story is an invention aimed at decrying the leaders of Banū Ḥanīfah.[78] It is possible to discount some details which are obviously additions by story-tellers and which were meant to belittle Musaylimah. But, on the whole, Balādhurī's account enables us to suppose that the prophet sent a letter to Hawdhah suggesting an alliance of the *munāṣarah* type. Hawdhah delegated a deputation of prominent leaders of Banū Ḥanīfah to negotiate with Muḥammad. Their demands were not acceptable to him, and no agreement was concluded.

When Hawdhah died shortly after the correspondence between him and Muhammad had taken place, he was succeeded by Musaylimah, who apparently did not enjoy the same prestige and support from Persia. A small section of Banū Ḥanīfah, probably nomadic, antagonized him and leaned towards Muḥammad.[79] This section was led by Thumāmah b. Uthāl, who played a useful role on the side of the Muslims during the Riddah.

The tradition speaks of further contacts between Muḥammad and Musaylimah. There is enough evidence to suspect many of the traditional reports concerning Musaylimah; but,

[73]Athīr, II, 215.

[74]Isḥāq, 998; Sa'd, I/II, 55; *Fut.*, I, 105; Ṭab., I, 1738; see also *E. I.*, article "Musailima" by F. Buhl.

[75]Athīr, II, 215.

[76]Bal. *Fut.*, I, 105.

[77]Watt, 134.

[78]Caetani, *Annali*, II/I, 336 (notes 1, 3).

[79]Watt, 133.

even if we accept them at face value, they still do not mention any agreements concluded between the two leaders. On the contrary, all signs indicate that Musaylimah, supported by the overwhelming majority of Banū Ḥanīfah, declared his opposition to Muḥammad before the latter's death. We do not have any evidence to the effect that any part of Banū Ḥanīfah had paid or agreed to pay any tax to Medina. Nowhere do we find any mention of any member of Banū Ḥanīfah taking part in Muḥammad's campaigns. Muḥammad's control over Banū Ḥanīfah was nil.

2) *The Tribes to the Northeast of Medina*

The area immediately to the northeast of Medina was inhabited by a conglomeration of nomadic tribes—Asad, Ṭayyi', Ghaṭafān, over which Muḥammad never did firmly establish control during his own lifetime.[80]

The most conspicuous feature of the situation in that area was the disintegration of the tribes into smaller clans and the complexity of the alliances among them.[81] Around the time of Muḥammad, we do not find among these tribes a leader of the stature of Hawdhah. These clans were outside the sphere of influence of either Persia or the Byzantines. Between these tribes, because of their bloody battles, animosity was strong.[82] And this animosity was a significant factor in their dealings with Muḥammad.[83]

The most frequently mentioned clan among this group—in relation to Muḥammad—is Fazārah, a section of Ghaṭafān. It seems to have been the largest and the strongest of them. 'Uyaynah b. Ḥiṣn, the leader of Fazārah, fought both against and on the side of Muḥammad. In the siege on Medina, he

[80] Watt, 81, 87-95.
[81] Watt, 78, 81; Sa'd, I/II, 23; Kaḥḥālah (see Biblo.), 689.
[82] Ya'qūbī, I, 230; Kaḥḥālah, 738-739, 402, 918-919, 690; Watt, 88, 91.
[83] Ṭabarī, I, 1893; Watt, 88.

was allied with the Meccans.[84] In the conquest of Mecca and Ḥunayn, he was allied with the Muslims. 'Uyaynah was one of the frequently mentioned *mu'allafah qulubuhum*, whose hearts were reconciled to Islam.[85] There is no record of his becoming Muslim during Muḥammad's lifetime, except in Ibn 'Abd al-Barr, who claims that 'Uyaynah adopted Islam after the conquest of Mecca.[86] His relations with Muḥammad indicate that he and his clansmen were willing to join in any booty-promising battle. His conduct in al-Khandaq, in Ḥunayn, and in Khaybar[87] befitted an independent chief whose main interest was to look after his own. He bargained with his allies about his remuneration beforehand and, once the battle was over, he returned with his warriors to their territory and kept their freedom of action, which is typical of the *munāṣarah* alliance. After Ḥunayn we do not hear of 'Uyaynah until Muḥammad's death. His position, probably, declined a good deal during the last two years of the prophet's lifetime. The deputation to Medina from Fazārah came without 'Uyaynah.[88] Muḥammad seems to have succeeded in attracting some chiefs of that tribe to his side, thereby weakening 'Uyaynah's position and neutralizing him; but he could not win him over.

The tribe of Ṭayyi' became closer to Muḥammad because of its rivalries with Fazārah and Asad, its neighbors.[89] Muḥammad's letters to the various clans to Ṭayyi' share the same tone: of his support to them against their neighbors, especially Asad.[90] But, among Asad, only a negligible minority, ini-

[84] Isḥāq, 701; Wāqidī, 477; Sa'd, II/I' 47; Abū 'Ubayd, 161; Bal. *Ans.*, I, 343; Athīr, II, 178.

[85] Wāqidī, 946; Rāzī, Tafsīr, XVI, 111 (K. IX:60); Nuwayrī, XVII, 340; Ḥalabī, III, 85.

[86] Watt, 94; Ibn 'Abd al-Barr, *Istī'āb*, 1249.

[87] Watt, 92-94.

[88] Watt, 94; Diyārbakrī, II, 197.

[89] Watt, 88, 89.

[90] Sa'd, I/II, 23.

mical to Ṭalḥah, the most prominent leader in Asad, leaned toward Muḥammad.[91] This minority was led by Dirār b. al-Azwar, an early convert to Islam. Nonetheless, on the arrival of the news of the prophet's death, all Asad shifted to Ṭalḥah's side; so did the majority of Ṭayyi'.[92]

As regards Muḥammad's gaining control over this area, it seems that he died before the completion of his task. During the years 8 and 9, he played the chiefs of that area one against the other. Some portions of the tribes, probably sizable, tended to ally themselves with him. But his control over this area was tenuous. His rising power in the Ḥijāz left these weak tribes to the northeast with little choice but to join him. They were gradually drifting towards Medina, most probably unwillingly. The death of the prophet gave them the opportunity to regain their freedom and rid themselves of Medina's sway.

3) *Tamīm*

The tribe of Tamīm was scattered over the region between Yamāmah and Ḥīrah.[93] At this juncture of its history, the tribe was divided into many small groups led by jealous and rival chiefs.[94] It seems to have been jealousies among the chiefs rather than the small punitive raid[95] carried out by Uyaynah b. Ḥiṣn against a small section of Tamīm that brought Tamīm's deputation to Medina in the year 9 to consider the advantages of an alliance. Once one section of the tribe had sent a deputation to Muḥammad, the others followed example so as to forestall any advantage gained by that section over the others. It is also possible that Muḥammad's booty-promising military activity, rather than Islam,

[91]Watt, 88.
[92]Ṭab., I, 1892.
[93]Naqā'iḍ, I, 66; Ibn 'Abd Rabbih, II, 10, 20; Watt, 137.
[94]Ṭab., I, 1909; Wellhausen, *Skizzen*, VI, 12.
[95]Watt, 137.

had enchanted some of the Tamīmī chiefs, for the fact that some allied themselves to Muḥammad caused others to seek the same objective. The tribe, however, did not formally adopt Islam during Muḥammad's lifetime.[96]

* * *

Thus, we can conclude that in Najd—the area to the east and northeast of Medina, Muḥammad's control was far from entrenched during his lifetime. The rivalling, weak tribes of this area probably could do nothing other than yield to Muḥammad's pressure. They were drifting towards Medina without any employment of force. Their local rivalries were the most significant factor in their relation and behavior towards Muḥammad. Their relative distance from Medina allowed them a greater degree of freedom and ability to maneuver than tribes in the Ḥijāz had, and the motives behind some groups' alliances with Muḥammad explain their shifting allegiance. Muḥammad did not have direct control over these allies of his; their own chieftains remained in complete authority over their affairs. The death of Muḥammad and the squabbles among his followers over selection of a caliph encouraged these groups to sever whatever ties they had had with Medina.

THE COASTAL AREAS

The coastal parts of Arabia—Baḥrayn, 'Umān, and Yemen—had for a long time been under Persian rule.[97] In Baḥrayn and 'Umān, local chiefs ruled the Arab tribes in the name of the Persian king.[98] In Yemen, the Persian *Abnā'*, sons of Persian fathers and Arab mothers, constituted the ruling

[96] *E.I.*, article "al-Aḥnaf b. Qays" by Ch. Pellat; Watt, 139-140.

[97] Caetani, *Annali*, II/I, 193-203, 208-210, 456-458, 661-672; Watt, 117-132.

[98] Ibn Ḥabīb, 263; Bal. *Fut*, I, 95; Ibn al-Anthīr, II, 215.

class.[99] As long as the Persian Empire was strong and supported its agents in these areas, the tribes did not dare challenge their authority; but the wars between the Byzantines and the Persians and the defeat of the Persians had lowered the prestige of these "mulūk" and had deprived them of the source of their power. Consequently, the tribes rose against them, striving for independence. These tribes may have revolted against new taxes levied by the Persians as a result of their wars.

In Baḥrayn at this time there were three Arab tribes: 'Abd al-Qays, Bakr b. Wā'il, and part of Tamīm. In addition, Persians and Jews were living there.[100] Over the Arabs ruled al-Mundhir b. Sāwā, most probably from Tamīm.[101] He is usually mentioned in the sources among the six "mulūk" to whom Muḥammad sent letters after al-Ḥudaybiyah. The sources add that he, together with all the Arabs in Baḥrayn, adopted Islam and al-'Alā' b. al-Ḥaḍramī was the envoy of the prophet to Baḥrayn to collect the tax.[102]

In 'Umān, the tribe of al-Azd was dominant and a "malik" ruled over the tribe. At the time of Muḥammad, the two sons of al-Julandā from Banū al-Mustakhir were the rulers in 'Umān.[103] According to the traditional sources, the prophet delegated 'Amr. b. al-'Aṣ in the year 8 to call the Azd to Islam; they responded and 'Amr remained there to collect the tax.[104]

In Yemen, the rule of the Abnā' by this time was limited to

[99]Wellhausen, *Skizzen*, VI, 27; Caetani, Annali, II/I, 662-3; Watt, 118.

[100]Bal. *Fut.*, I, 95; Wellhausen, *Skizzen*, VI, 20; Watt, 131.

[101]Ibn Ḥabīb, 265; Bal. *Fut.*, I, 95; Ṭab., I, 1561; Caetani, *Annali*, II/I, 194.

[102]Ibn Ḥabīb, 77, 126; Sa'd, I/II, 19; 19; Bal. *Fut.*, I, 95; Ṭab. 1, I, 1561; Athīr, II, 215; Diyārbakrī, II, 183.

[103]Ibn Ḥabīb, 265; Sa'd, I/II, 18; Bal. *Fut.*, i, 92; Athīr, II, 272; Caetani, *Annali*, II/I, 206; Watt, 131.

[104]Ibn Ḥabīb, 77; Sa'd, I/II, 18; Bal. *Fut.*, I, 92; Ṭab., I, 1561; Caetani, *Annali*, 206-210.

Ṣan'ā'. Among the large number of tribes in Yemen and Ḥaḍramawt, we do not find outstanding leaders, even of the stature of 'Uyaynah of Fazārah.[105] Our sources present us with a long list of deputations from Yemen to Medina; they adopted Islam and the prophet delegated envoys to these tribes to teach them the *Koran* and collect the tax.[106] We are also told that the head of the Abnā' was the first to adopt Islam and that the prophet confirmed him in his governorship.[107]

Al-Mundhir b. Sāwā in Baḥrayn, Jayfar and 'Abbād, sons of al-Julandā in 'Umān, and the Abnā' in Yemen all faced the same problem. They had lost their power and prestige as a consequence of the lack of support they were getting from their confusion-stricken old master, Persia. Their authority was challenged by local, rival chiefs who probably wielded more power than they—such as, al-Ḥuṭam in Baḥrayn, Laqīt in 'Umān, and al-Aswad in Yemen. These troubled agents of the Persians were the people with whom Muḥammad dealt. They were looking for outside help and support to keep their position and most probably contacted Muḥammad of their own accord.[108] Since Persia could not offer the badly needed support to these agents, they accepted Muḥammad's nominal backing. No Muslim armies were sent to these areas during Muḥammad's lifetime; he satisfied himself with the delegation of a few agents as token of his support.

It is probable that these "mulūk" found it more advantageous to transfer the *itāwah* they used to pay to the Persian king to Muḥammad.[109] But it is doubtful whether any of these regions, other than Christian Najrān, paid any tax to Muḥammad. The hurried manner in which Muḥammad's

[105]Wellhausen, *Skizzen*, VI, 26-27, Caetani, *Annali*, II/I, 661-667; Watt, 117-118.

[106]Isḥāq, 1002-1010; Sa'd, III, 59-86; Bal. *Fut.*, I, 82; Ṭabarī, I, 1717; Diyārbakrī, II, 194-198.

[107]Ṭab., I, 1575, 1851, 1852; Ibn Sayyid al-Nās, II, 263-264.

[108]Ṭab., I, 1574-75; Ibn Sayyid al-Nās, II, 263-64.

[109]R. Blachère, *Le Problème de Mahomet*, 120.

agents fled these areas when, shortly after his death, the revolt against them and their allies erupted indicates the weakness of those allies and their lack of power to stand against the tribal upheaval. By the time these "mulūk" had concluded agreements with the prophet, they were no longer in control of their areas, as later events during the so-called "Wars of al-Riddah" would prove. Practically in every one of these places, the party allied with the Muslims was on the defensive, and the overwhelming majority of the tribes were on the side of the "rebels". Under these circumstances, it is impossible to assert that these areas were brought under Muḥammad's control during his lifetime.

THE NORTH

> Abū Umāmah al-Bāhilī said: "I have heard the Messenger of God say, 'Verily God has turned my face towards al-Shām and my back toward Yemen and said to me: O Muḥammad! I have made what is behind you a reinforcement for you and what faces you a booty and livelihood.' "[110]

After the capitulation of Mecca and the surrender of the Ḥijāz, the north[111] and the route to the Syrian Desert claimed Muḥammad's greatest attention.[112] Arabia, outside of the Ḥijāz, was not of much concern to him. He probably foresaw its surrender to him, without fighting, if the strife between the tribes continued. While no army was sent by Muḥammad to Yemen or Yamāmah (even when the news of the rising of al-Aswad and Musaylimah, in each of those two areas respectively, reached him), Muḥammad led the biggest reported campaign to Tabūk himself.

From al-Hūdaybiyah on, Muḥammad concentrated his

[110] Ibn 'Asākir, I, 378 ff.

[111] M. J. de Goeje, *Mémoire sur la conquête de la Syrie*, 1-20; Caetani, *Annali*, II/I, 80-88; Watt, 105-117.

[112] Watt, 105.

main military activity in the north on the route to Syria. In the year 7 (628 A.D.), he attacked and seized Khaybar. Immediately following Khaybar's fall, other Jewish colonies —Fadak, Wādī al-Qurā, and Taymā'—surrendered and were granted the same terms as those granted Khaybar.[113] In the year 8, Muḥammad sent an expedition to Mu'tah under the command of Zayd b. Ḥārith. The expedition did not materialize in recognizable success. Zayd and two other prominent Muslims were killed, and the army returned to Medina.[114] Muḥammad also dispatched another expedition to Dhāt al-Salāsil under the command of the famous 'Amr b. al-'Aṣ and reinforced him with a detachment which included some of the most prominent companions, Abū Bakr, 'Umar, and Abū 'Ubaydah.[115] In the year 9, the prophet himself led a campaign to Tabūk.[116] Before his death, he had prepared another expedition to Syria under the command of Usāmah b. Zayd, which was dispatched by Abū Bakr.[117] In addition to these major campaigns, there were quite a few other smaller ones such as that under the command of Khālid b. al-Walīd to Dūmat al-Jandal.[118]

It was a few months after the capitulation of Mecca that Muḥammad led the biggest reported campaign of his lifetime: to Tabūk. The traditional sources speak at length of the difficulties which Muḥammad encountered in recruiting an army for the campaign to Tabūk and in supplying it with minimum equipment.[119] This army is known traditionally as *jaysh al-'usrah,* the army of distress, because of all the difficulties which faced Muḥammad in its preparation. The sources

[113]Bal. *Ans.*, 352; Watt, 218.
[114]Watt, 53-55.
[115]Balādhurī, *Ans.*, I, 380.
[116]Bal. *Ans.*, I, 368; Watt, 105-106.
[117]Bal. *Ans.*, I, 384.
[118]Bal. *Ans.*, I, 382; Athīr, II, 281.
[119]Isḥāq, 943 ff.; Wāqidī, 990 ff.; Sa'd, II/I, 120; Bal. *Ans.*, I, 368; Ṭab., I, 1693; Athīr, II, 276-278.

speak of antagonism to Muḥammad and of dissention in the Muslim camp.[120] They are silent or vague, however, as to the purpose of this difficult and costly campaign and, also, as to the reasons behind Muḥammad's return to Medina without having achieved his goal.

The sources are not agreed, vague as they may be, on the motives behind this campaign to the Syrian border. According to some, it was the news that reached Medina of the impending invasion of Arabia by Heraclius that evoked this response.[121] Others, however, are silent about the intent or ascribe it to a revelation; these sources seem to be based on the works of al-Zuhrī, which are no longer extent.[122] An interesting version of the story, on the authority of Ibn ʿAbbās, runs as follows: "The prophet remained [in Medina] six months after his return from Ṭā'if. God then ordered him to attack Tabūk. This campaign is the one God called 'the hour of distress', *sāʿat al-ʿusrah.* It was in very hot weather when hypocrisy [*nifāq*], had spread and the *aṣḥāb al-ṣuffah* became many."[123] The terms *nifāq* and *munāfiqūn* are used by the sources to designate "opposition" and "opponents" to Muḥammad in the Muslim camp.[124] Concerning the *aṣḥāb al-ṣuffah,* a comment is infixed in the text to the effect that they were the poor among the Muslims who lived on the contributions of the prophet and the Muslims. The Muslims used to supply them with provisions and take them on raids as a charitable deed in the service of God.[125]

The story that the campaign to Tabūk was a response to Heraclius' intention of invading Arabia should be discounted.

[120] Isḥāq, 946 ff.; Wāqidī, 1003 ff., 1042 ff.; Ṭab., I, 1699-1701; Athīr, II, 278.

[121] Sa'd, II/I, 119; Bal. *Ans.*, I, 368; Athīr, II, 277; ʿAsākir, I, 413.

[122] Isḥāq, 943; Ṭab., I, 1693; ʿAsākir, I, 412; concerning al-Zuhrī and his works, cf. A. A. Dūrī, *Nash'at ʿilm al-tārīkh ʿind al-Arab*, 23-25.

[123] ʿAsākir, I, 408.

[124] Cf., Watt, 180.

[125] ʿAsākir, I, 408.

If this were true, why then did not Muḥammad carry out his plans to their end? If Muḥammad were ready for an encounter with the far superior Byzantine army, would he not drag that army to the desert and force it fight under adverse conditions? Muḥammad certainly knew of the victory that Heraclius had just won over the Persians, and he was aware of the superiority of the Byzantine army over his own.[126] It is more credible that the presence of Heraclius in Ḥimṣ at that time is what deterred Muḥammad from venturing further into Syria.

Ibn 'Abbās' version suggests that there were many poor among the Muslims and that Muḥammad did not have the resources to provide for them. At first the Muhājirūn were few and the Anṣār supported them. Now, nine years had elapsed; the number of have-not Muslims in Medina had grown considerably, and the Anṣār did not welcome the situation. Many references to the bitterness of the Anṣār about the situation in their town are found in the *diwān* of Ḥassān b. Thābit, the poet of the prophet.[127] The *aṣḥāb al-ṣuffah* bring to mind the *ṣa'ālīk* phenomenon in Arabia. According to *al-Aghānī*, the *ṣa'ālīk* were groups of brigands who rallied around a leader from among themselves and lived on plunder.[128] Indeed, among the early followers of Muḥammad we find people of the *ṣa'ālīk*-type such as 'Amr b. Umayyah al-Ḍamrī.[129] These seem to be the people Ibn 'Abbās meant by *aṣḥāb al-ṣuffah.*

This same story of Ibn 'Abbās tells of the spread of hypocrisy in Medina. It became remarkable following the capitulation of Mecca and subsequent battle of Ḥunayn. The Anṣār were irritated by the behavior of the prophet during the campaign on Mecca. They seem to have looked forward

[126] 'Asākir, I, 413.
[127] Ḥassān b. Thābit al-Anṣārī, *Sharḥ diwān*, ed. al-Barqūqī, 104.
[128] *Aghānī*, III, 70-83 (biography of 'Urwah b. al-Ward).
[129] Athīr, II, 169; Ibn Sayyid al-Nās, II, 112; see also, Ya'qūbī, II, 78.

to setting old accounts with the Meccans. The prophet, through the intercession of Abū Sufyān, shattered these hopes of the Anṣār.[130] The traditional sources speak at length of the disappointment of the Anṣār as regards Muḥammad's deferential treatment of the newly converted Meccans after the battle of Ḥunayn.[131] The Anṣār returned to their town empty-handed after a booty-promising campaign to Mecca and Ṭā'if. This, coupled with the favoritism with which the prophet treated the Meccans, certainly was exploited by the "hypocrites" in Medina for the purpose of deprecating his faithful followers.

With these problems confronting him, Muḥammad resolved to attack the Arab tribes in the Syrian Desert, who were the primary target of the campaign to Tabūk. Granted the success of such an astute move, the campaign to Tabūk would supply *aṣḥāb al-ṣuffah* with their needs, compensate the Anṣār for their dissatisfaction with the conquest of Mecca and the battle of Ḥunayn, and satisfy the Quraysh who had lost their trade.

The prophet encountered much difficulty in preparing for the campaign to Tabūk. His financial resources were not sufficient to help those who wanted to take part but could not themselves afford the expenses, so he keenly urged the Muslims to contribute with generosity to help finance this campaign. The tradition extols those among the rich companions who responded to the prophet's plea. 'Uthmān is reported to have equipped a third of this army, the number of which is given as thirty-thousand.[132] The participants in this army were from Medina, Mecca, and the tribes of the surrounding areas.[133]

[130]Isḥāq, 865; Wāqidī, 822; Sa'd, II/I, 98; Ibn Qutaybah, *Ma'ārif*, 163, Bayhaqī, *Sunan*, IX, 117.

[131]Isḥāq, 934-5; Sa'd, II/I, 111; Ṭab., I, 1683-84; Athīr, II, 271; Ibn Abī al-Ḥadīd, VI, 22-26; cf., also Watt, 180-191.

[132]Isḥāq, 945; Wāqidī, 996; Sa'd, II/I, 119; Ṭabarī, II, 1694; Athīr, II, 277; 'Asākir, I, 414.

[133]Caetani, *Annali*, II/I, 240.

At Tabūk the prophet realized that with such a poorly-equipped army, far away from home, he could not risk an encounter with the Byzantines or their Arab allies. The memory of Mu'tah, where he lost his adopted son Zayd and his cousin Ja'far, was still alive in his mind. He could not afford another disaster like that. The campaign to Tabūk seems to have been a pre-mature attempt to invade Syria. It made an impressive show of power, however, which induced some localities on the Syrian border to conclude treaties with Muḥammad and pay him a tribute.[134] This, in addition to some alliances with small Arab tribes on the border, was the extent of Muḥammad's control in the north.[135] The major tribes in Syria, like Ghassān, Bahrā' and Lakhm, remained antagonistic to him.[136]

* * *

On his arrival in Medina, Muḥammad started to prepare for a bigger and better-equipped campaign against Syria. Immediately following Tabūk, we notice a drastic change in Muḥammad's policy towards his allies. In that same year, 9 A.H., a revelation is said to have come to him—to impose an obligatory tax on those who sought his support.[137] The tax is called *ṣadaqah* both in Koranic verse and in the sources which refer to it. It was later called *ṣadaqah* or *zakāt*. But the name of this tax is only of minor importance compared with the broader significance: of such a move by Muḥammad at this particular time, of the nature of this tax, and of its implications regarding relations between Muḥammad and his would-be allies.

This was the year 9 A.H., i.e., a year after the surrender of Mecca, the year of the failure of Tabūk, and the "year of

[134]Sa'd, II/I; Bal. *Fut.*, I, 71-75; Athīr, II, 280-81.
[135]Watt, 109-110.
[136]Cf. also, Faysal, *Ḥarakāt*, 26-27.
[137]*Koran*, IX:104; Sa'd, II/I, 115; Ṭab., I, 1722; Mas'ūdi, 237.

deputations." At this point Muḥammad was strong enough to impose his will in Arabia but not strong enough to fight the Byzantines in Syria; and, having the opportunity of dictating his terms to all those who sought to ally themselves with him, he exploited that opportunity and imposed the tax. This tax, as later events during the Riddah demonstrate, was supposed to be an obligatory, yearly levy. The nearby tribes, around Medina, helpless against Muḥammad's rising power, yielded to his requisitions and looked forward to an auspicious moment—to break that agreement.

Ibn Sa'd gives a list of names of tax collectors and of the tribes to which they were sent.[138] The list indicates that only those tribes in the Ḥijāz and northeast of Medina, if any, were asked to pay the tax during the year 9. There is, however, no recorded instance wherein it is mentioned that this tax was paid during Muḥammad's lifetime. The most plausible explanation for this matter is that although the revelation for the imposition of the tax came in the year 9, it was not announced to the tribes until the end of the year, during the pilgrimage period, when they congregated in the sanctuary of Mecca. If so, then the collectors were sent each to his destination during the year 10. And, before these agents of Muḥammad had returned with the tax to Medina, he died—at the beginning of the year 11. This explanation is supported by the sequence of events during the last year of the prophet's lifetime and the beginning of Abū Bakr's caliphate.

At the end of the year 9, Abū Bakr led the Muslims in pilgrimage.[139] According to the tradition, *Surat al-Barā'ah* ("freedom from responsibility") was revealed to the prophet after the departure of Abū Bakr. 'Alī was delegated to bring the message to all those—Muslims and non-Muslims—who came to the sanctuary in Mecca that year.[140]

[138] Sa'd, II/I, 115.

[139] Isḥāq, 970; Wāqidī, 1076; Ṭab., I, 1720; Mas'ūdī, 237; Athīr, II, 291.

[140] Isḥāq, 972; Wāqidī, 1077; Ṭab., I, 1720; Athīr, II, 291.

Surat al-Barā'ah, also known as *Surat al-Tawbah* ("repentance"), runs as follows:

> An acquittal, from God and His Messenger, unto the idolators with whom you made covenant: 'Journey freely in the land for four months; and know that you cannot frustrate the will of God, and that God degrades the unbelievers.'
> A proclamation, from God and His Messenger, unto mankind on the day of the Greater Pilgrimage: 'God is quit, and His Messenger, of the idolators. So if you repent, that will be better for you; but if you turn your backs, know that you cannot frustrate the will of God. And give thou good tidings to the unbelievers of a painful chastisement;
> excepting those of the idolators with whom you made covenant, then they failed you naught neither lent them support to any man against you. With them fulfill your covenant till their term; surely God loves the godfearing. Then, when the sacred months are drawn away, slay the idolators wherever you find them, and take them and confine them, and lie in wait for them at every place of ambush. But if they repent, and perform the prayer, and pay the alms, then let them go their way.[141]

Surat al-Barā'ah indicates a stringent change in Muḥammad's policy towards non-Muslim Arabs. The old agreements which did not carry any obligations would be terminated soon and only complete submission to the authority of Muḥammad would be tolerated. Non-muslims would not be allowed to visit the sanctuary any more and would be killed wherever they be found. This also indicates that Muḥammad found himself powerful enough at this time to present the tirbes with such demands. The fact that he entrusted his most prominent follower, Abū Bakr, and his cousin 'Alī with the

[141] *Koran*, IX:1-6 (Tr. by A. J. Arberry), *The Koran Interpreted*, 207.

mission of bringing the ultimatum to the knowledge of the tribes indicates the gravity of the matter.

Muḥammad's change of policy and the pressure he brought to bear on the tribes left them with the choice either to submit completely to his authority or to take to arms against him. This seems to be what actually happened during the following year. The weaker tribes, who could not stand the pressure, gave in and unwillingly agreed to pay the tax; the stronger ones defied his ultimatum and stood up in open hostility towards him. While, during the year 10, delegations streamed to Medina; al-Aswad in Yemen, Musaylimah in Yamāmah, and Ṭalḥah in Asad all declared their animosity to Muḥammad, to his allies, and to his religion during his lifetime.[142]

In the year 10, Muḥammad led the pilgrimage himself, apparently to stress fruther what Abū Bakr had proclaimed the year before. This was the famous *Hijjat al-Wadā'*, Farewell Pilgrimage, a few months after which the prophet died. Shortly before his death, he had prepared an expedition to Syria under the command of Usāmah, the son of Zayd b. Hārithah.[143] In that army, according to the tradition, were the most prominent of the early Muhājirūn; Abū Bakr, 'Umar, and Abū 'Ubaydah were put under the command of the eighteen-year old Usāmah.[144] There was widespread complaint among the Muslims about the appointment of Usāmah to the command of such a campaign. The prophet died before Usāmah and his army had departed from Medina,[145] and his death had great repercussions on the ensuing events in Arabia. These made themselves felt not only on Usāmah's campaign but also on the tax, which Muḥammad had imposed and

[142]Isḥāq, 1018; al-Ya'qūbī, II, 130; Bal. *Fut.*, 105, 125; Ṭab. I, 1749, 1795, 1797; Athīr, II, 337, 343; Diyārbakrī, II, 155, 157.

[143]Isḥāq, 1056; Ya'qūbī, II, 113; Sa'd, II/I, 136; Bal. *Ans.*, 384; Ṭab., I, 1794-5; Mas'ūdī, 241; 'Asākir, I, 423-427.

[144]Isḥāq, 1056; Sa'd, II/I, 136; Ṭab., I, 1794; Mas'ūdī, 241; Ibn al-Athīr, II, 317, 'Asākir, I, 426.

[145]See sources listed in note 140.

was so anxious to see established and functioning among the tribes. Since he died before his agents had returned to Medina with the first year's tax, and the tribes had seized the occasion of his death to withhold it; it was, thus, the first year's regular and obligatory tax that Abū Bakr insisted on procuring, even by force, from the tribes. This is discussed in greater detail in the next chapter.

2. THE ELECTION OF ABU BAKR

The importance, in a study of al-Riddah, of what happened in Medina immediately after Muḥammad's death—and why an entire chapter of this book is devoted to the election of Abū Bakr—is that the constellation of interests which thrust Abū Bakr into the foremost position of power in Arabia were virtually the same as powered the various campaigns commonly called the wars of apostasy. In this chapter, attention will be drawn to the point that, although interest groups spoke up in Medina for various candidates, no single group was organized enough to be called a party. The only candidate having anything at all resembling a program was Abū Bakr; it was that he could be trusted to follow in the political footsteps of his late mentor, Muḥammad. Among the contending groups in Medina, there were, of course, those who did not want a continuation of Muḥammad's ways, especially of the favoritism he bestowed on newly-converted Meccans to the detriment of Anṣār and Muhājirūn alike. How this embroilment of interests was resolved in the election of Abū Bakr was not just an event which preceded the wars of al-Riddah; the election of Abū Bakr *ensured* that they would be fought.

* * *

The questions as to whether the prophet had nominated a successor and who that nominee might have been have long been, and still are, matters of dispute between the Shī'ah and Sunnah sects of Islam. Whatever the correct answers may be, the prevalent opinion among historians today is that there is no evidence that Muḥammad made any provisions before he died for a government to rule the Muslim state he had established in Medina.[1] What is certain is that, following Muḥammad's death, the Muslim community in Medina suffered serious rupture. It split into groups contending for the succession to the prophet's political position. Each of the rival groups claimed that one of its members was the rightful heir to the vacant position.

It is a well-known episode in the annals of Islam that no sooner was the prophet dead than the Anṣār held a meeting to deliberate about a successor and ended by proclaiming one of their members caliph. This action, of course, was inacceptable to the Muhājirūn who, as a whole, held the view that they were more entitled to the position. Within the Muhājirūn, the tradition claims, there was a faction of the prophet's kinsmen and their followers who viewed themselves as legitimate heirs to the authority "their man" had established. The frictions between these three contending groups brought the community to the brink of fratricidal strife.[2] The prevalent view among the historians of this early period of Islam is that the foregoing crisis was averted only by the resolute action undertaken by three prominent members of the early companions of the prophet—Abū Bakr, Abū 'Ubaydah, and 'Umar—and that the success of their resolution was facilitated by the jealousies among the Anṣār.[3] This view is based on the Sunni tradition that the three companions, as it is told,

[1]Arnold, *The Caliphate*, 19; Lewis, 50; Watt, *Islamic Political Thought* (Islamic Surveys 6), Edinburgh, 1968, 31.

[2]Caetani, *Chro.*, I, 110; Lewis, 50-51; Muir, *The Caliphate*, 1.

[3]Muir, 2-4; Caetani, *Chro.*, 110; Lewis, 51; see also H. Lamens' "Le triumvirat...", 113-144.

rushed to the meeting-place of the Anṣār, put down the agitation, and carried away the assembled people to elect Abū Bakr caliph. This was to have taken place on the same day the prophet died.[4] On the following day, the news of the new caliph was published in the mosque, whereupon Abū Bakr arose to deliver his traditionally well-known speech.[5] 'Alī, cousin and son-in-law of the prophet, refrained from giving his oath of allegiance, *bay'ah*, to the new caliph.

In general, the traditional sources paint a grim picture of the political scene in Medina following the death of Muḥammad. One of the descriptions runs as follows:

> When Abū Bakr was given the *bay'ah* [the act by which a person is proclaimed and recognized head of the Muslim state],[6] and he rallied the Anṣār around the affair concerning which [the Muslims] had split, he said: "Let the expedition of Usāmah be carried out." At this point the Arabs had apostatized, tribes as a whole or in part, hypocrisy sprouted, Jews and Christians rose up their heads. The Muslims were like sheep on a rainy night because they had lost their prophet and because of their sparsity and the multitude of their enemy. People then said to [Abū Bakr]: "[The army of Usāmah] are the bulk of the Muslims and the Arabs have revolted against you; you ought not dispense with the Muslim community around you." Abū Bakr replied: "By Him in whose hands is the soul of Abū Bakr, if I were to be torn by predatory beasts, I would still dispatch the expedition of Usāmah, as the prophet ordered, and if I were to be left alone in these dwellings, I would still send it to its destination."[7]

[4]Caetani, *Chro.*, I, 110; Lewis, 51.

[5]Caetani, *Chro.*, I, 110.

[6]*E. I.*, article "Bay'ah" by E. Tyan; cf. also by E. Tyan, *Institutions du Droit Public Musulman*, I, 315-321.

[7]Bal. *Fut.*, 114; Ṭab., I, 1848; for comparable descriptions, see also Mas'ūdī, 247; Athīr, II, 334.

THE ANṢĀR

During the last few years of the prophet's lifetime, the Anṣār had been deeply disappointed in the favoritism Muḥammad had displayed towards the newly-converted Quraysh. In a series of events which had begun long before the prophet's death, the Anṣār had been persistent in their objection to the growing influence of the Meccans upon the policies of the Muslim state of Medina. Almost without exception, however, each time they tried anything, they were unable to achieve the control they sought. During the campaign to Mecca and at the time of its capitulation, the Anṣār were frustrated by the arrangement for a peaceful surrender of the town which the prophet had managed to effect. They had lost thereby the opportunity of settling old accounts with the Meccans and were deprived of the chance to win a booty-promising battle against their wealthy enemy. Furthermore, the Anṣār were disheartened by the prophet's deferential treatment of his newly-converted compatriots. After the victory in Ḥunayn, the Anṣār were distressed to see others, who only yesterday had been the bitter enemies of Islam, gathering the fruits of what they considered their own toil. Large prizes from the Ḥunayni booty went to newly-converted Meccans, and none of the Anṣārī chiefs got any. The Anṣār frowned on the prophet's conduct and indignantly expressed their emotions, but in the end they submitted to Muḥammad's will.[8]

Still bitter after Muḥammad's death, the Anṣār objected strongly to the election of Abū Bakr; and, for that matter, they would have objected with equal vehemence had any other Meccan been under consideration. Hence, while Muḥammad was lying dead in the house of 'A'ishah, the Anṣār convened in the *saqīfah*,[9] of Banū Sā'idah, a clan of the

[8]Isḥāq, 498-99; Wāqidi, 956 ff.; Sa'd, II/I, 111; Ibn Qutaybah, *Ma'ārif*, 163; Nuwayrī, XVII, 347.

[9]A *saqīfah* is a roofed hall in this context; it seems to have been a hall in which the clan used to hold its assemblies.

Khazraj tribe from Medina, and went about the business of nominating one of their numbers to be caliph.[10] Although the sources speak at length of the argument and bargaining between the Anṣār and the Muhājirūn, at the same time they deal with the jealousies among the Anṣār themselves—jealousies which caused them to lose the case. The convention of the Anṣār in that *saqīfah* and its proceedings is known in the tradition as the *Amr al-Saqīfah*, the affairs of the hall.[11] It was there that Abū Bakr eventually received the *bay'ah.* But the Anṣār did not forget their bitterness towards the Meccan aristocracy, whom now they held accountable also for Abū Bakr's election. After the election, they tokenly accepted his political authority but remained hostile, nonetheless, to him and his Meccan retinue. This is known from the poetry of Ḥassān b. Thābit al-Anṣārī, the mouthpiece and advocate of his group's cause. His satiric denunciation of Meccan aristocracy bears witness to that long-fostered hostility: Abū Sufyān, Suhayl b. 'Amr, al-Ḥārith b. Abī Sufyān, and 'Ikrimah b. Abī Jahl, the prominent leaders of the Meccan clans, were targets of his satire.[12]

During the caliphate of Abū Bakr, the Anṣār continued in their opposition to his policies. They complained about the campaign of Usāmah and contributed much to its failure.[13] During the war in Arabia, the Anṣār were always reluctant to participate in the fighting.[14] Yet, in almost all cases, the Anṣār were compelled to abdicate their will to the Meccans, who, quite early in the game, succeeded in dominating this opposing

[10]*E. I.*, articles "Anṣār" by W. M. Watt; "Abū Bakr" by W. M. Watt; "'Alī" by L. Veccia Vaglieri.

[11]For the story of the *saqīfah*, see Isḥāq, 1071-1075; Ya'qūbī, II, 123-126; Bal. *Ans.*, I, 580-82; Ṭab., I, 1837-1845; Mas'ūdī, 247; Athīr, II, 325-332; Arnold, *op. cit.*, 19; Caetani, *Annali*, II/I, 510-518.

[12]Ibn Abī al-Ḥadīd, VI, 22-25. The *qaṣīdah* (ode) on p. 25 is not included in the *dīwān* of Ḥassān.

[13]Cf. below (Chapter IV) as to campaign of Usāmah.

[14]Cf. Chapter IV, regarding al-Buzākhah, al-Butāḥ, and 'Aqrabā'.

force. Frustrated as they were, the Anṣār allied themselves sympathetically with another opposition group, the party of 'Alī; and the two groups kept resentfully silent until the time of 'Uthmān, the third caliph.

MUḤAJIRŪN

Among the Muḥajirūn, there were three roughly distinguishable factions.

Of the prominent companions and kinsmen of the prophet, 'Alī, al-'Abbās, al-Zubayr, and Talḥah were for giving the *bay'ah* to 'Alī. They abstained from supporting Abū Bakr. Those who became known later as *Shī'at 'Alī*, the followers of 'Alī, claimed that the prophet had, prior to his death, announced his desire that 'Alī be his successor.[15] There is, however, no indication that this group worked actively to promote its cause. They yielded, likewise, to the authority of the new caliph. 'Alī's claims of legitimate right to the caliphate became a religious matter, and the traditions supporting it were accepted by the Shī'is as a matter of faith.

Another faction was headed by 'Umar, the arch-enemy of the Meccan aristocracy. 'Umar's first choice was Abū 'Ubaydah, for whom he apparently could not muster enough support. Because 'Umar did indeed make a strong effort to prevent Abū Bakr from being elected caliph and because Abū Bakr's strength was sufficient to negate 'Umar's efforts, a separate section will follow in which 'Umar's part in this election is studied closely.

The third faction of Muḥājirūn supported Abū Bakr. Abū Bakr's early conversion to Islam, his staunch support of the prophet, his kinship to him through 'A'ishah, his advanced age and experience and knowledge of Arab genealogies, and the fact that the prophet had entrusted him with heading the pilgrimage in the year 9 and with leading the prayer

[15]See D. M. Donaldson, *The Shi'ite Religion*, London, 1933, 1.

during the prophet's illness are all factors cited in explanation of Abū Bakr's victory.[16] But these attributes were also to be found in several others of the early companions. Why then was Abū Bakr chosen and none other? An analysis of the events in Medina following the death of the prophet demonstrates clearly that it was mainly the support of the newly-converted Meccan aristocracy that tipped the balance in Abū Bakr's favor.

It would be misleading to view the different groups in Medina in terms of political parties, each with its political platform and an agreed-upon candidate for the caliphate. Each party's maneuverings concentrated on forestalling the other's ambitions more than on promoting its own cause. This was the case with the Anṣār—who were agreed on preventing the Qurayshites from winning the caliphate but disagreed among themselves as to which of their members they should support. The 'Alids satisfied themselves with putting forward their claim to the right of inheriting the prophet's political position, but they did nothing actively to promote their cause. There is no indication that 'Umar pressed the matter of Abū 'Ubaydah and his candidacy for the caliphate beyond a certain point; but 'Umar was active in shattering the other groups' aspirations.

'UMAR'S PART IN THE ELECTION

As in the case of the Anṣārī opposition, the party of 'Umar had its beginnings in the last few years of the prophet's lifetime. The political activities of this group and their opposition to Abū Bakr and his policies are underplayed in the traditional sources. Muslim traditionists, in their attempt to present the early Muslim community as the ideal and an example that should be followed, suppressed much of the information about this group's activities. But enough has been left, scattered

[16]Cf., for example, Watt, *Islamic Political Thought*, 32.

incidentally in the sources, to indicate the existence of such an opposition group.

Ibn Abī al-Ḥadīd, for example, sets forth a series of incidents in which 'Umar stood in opposition to decisions taken by the prophet. Among several other minor incidents, the following episodes indicate a definite line of policy adopted by 'Umar: (1) After the victory in Badr, 'Umar insisted on having the Meccan captives executed. The prophet, however, supported by Abū Bakr, sought an agreement whereby these captives would be set free against ransom.[17] (2) In al-Ḥudaybiyah, 'Umar objected to the terms of that treaty, but the prophet ratified it anyway.[18] (3) During the campaign against Mecca—when Abū Sufyān arrived at the Muslim camp to negotiate with the prophet about the peaceful surrender of the town—'Umar objected to granting amnesty to the Umayyad leader and wanted to have him executed.[19] (4) When 'Abd Allah b. Ubayy, head of the "hypocrites" in Medina, died, 'Umar argued with the prophet that he should not pray for 'Abd Allah's soul.[20] Even so, the prophet did. These episodes demonstrate 'Umar's unrelenting stand for a non-compromisingly tough policy towards the influential leaders of the enemies of Islam, especially the Meccan aristocracy.

During the caliphate of Abū Bakr, 'Umar and his group objected to waging war against the Arab tribes and kept urging the caliph to discharge Khālid b. al-Wālid from the command of the Muslim army.[21] 'Umar opposed the appointment of the Umayyad Khālid b. Sa'īd as commander of an army that was dispatched to Syria, and he succeeded in re-

[17]Ibn Abī al-ḥadīd, XII, 60; the incidents compiled by this authoı are confirmed by others and are well-known in the tradition.

[18]*Ibid.*, 59.

[19]Ṭab., I, 1632.

[20]Ibn Abī al-Ḥadīd, XII, 55.

[21]Ṭab., I, 1900, 1926, 1928; Bal. *Fut.*, I, 116; Wathīmah, 12; *al-Aghānī*, XV, 239, 242, 244; Baghdādī, Khizānah, I, 238; Diyārbakrī, II, 209.

moving Khālid from that position.[22] Immediately after his succession to the caliphate, 'Umar discharged Khālid b. al-Wālid from the command of the Muslim army in Syria and appointed in his stead a close associate of his, an early companion, Abū 'Ubaydah.[23] Also, 'Umar tightened his grip on 'Amr b. al-'Aṣ in Egypt and confiscated half of his property.[24] As caliph, 'Umar discriminated against the Meccans in the '*atā*', stipend. In short, 'Umar tried his best to suppress the newly-converted Muslims of the Meccan aristocracy.[25]

In spite of these episodes showing 'Umar in disagreement with the prophet and the first caliph, the tradition usually presents Abū Bakr, 'Umar and Abū 'Ubaydah in complete harmony. Most sources are agreed that the three arrived together at the *saqīfah* of Banū Sā'idah and there proclaimed Abū Bakr caliph without ado.[26] Balādhurī, however, gives the following report:

> When the prophet died, 'Umar came to Abū 'Ubaydah and said: "Stretch your hand and let us give you the *bay'ah*, for you are the custodian (*amīn*) of this *ummah* (the Muslim community), as the prophet called you." Abū 'Ubaydah answered: "O 'Umar, since I adopted Islam I have not suspected your uprighteousness before. How would you give me the *bay'ah* while al-siddīq Abū Bakr is among you? and he was the second of the two" (in reference to Abū Bakr's flight with the prophet from Mecca and their hiding in the cave.).[27]

A scrutiny of another report given in Ṭabarī on the authority

[22] 'Asākir, 448, 454.
[23] De Goege, *Mémoir*, 64-70.
[24] Ibn Abī al-Ḥadīd, XII, 55.
[25] Cf. also Ṭāhā Ḥusayn, *al-Fitnah al-Kubrā*, I, 79-83.
[26] Ya'qūbī, II, 123-126; Bal. *Ans*, I, 580-582; Ṭab., I, 1817-30; Ibn Qutaybah, *al-Imāmah wa-al-Siyāsah*, 4-8; Ibn Abī al-Ḥadīd, VI, 11-26.
[27] Bal. *Ans.*, I, 579.

of Ibn 'Abbās[28] reveals that 'Umar was not for the election of Abū Bakr until the last minute. Ibn 'Abbās claimed to have heard the story from 'Umar himself, who in the mosque of Medina narrated the happenings on the day of Abū Bakr's election. 'Umar is reported to have said: "It reached me that some of you (Muslims) say: "If the caliph dies he would give the *bay'ah* to so-and-so (a reference to 'Alī). Let nobody be deceived by the saying that 'the *bay'ah* to Abū Bakr was a *faltah* (an unexpected event with regrettable consequences).' Truly it was so, but God safeguarded us against its calamitous consequences. Furthermore, among you there is no one of Abū Bakr's like." 'Umar then proceeded to tell how he, Abū Bakr, and Abū 'Ubaydah arrived in the *saqīfah* where the Anṣār were assembled ready to proclaim one of their own members caliph. He recalled the arguments which had gone on between the Anṣār and the three of them. He claimed that Abū Bakr had offered to give the *bay'ah* to either one who would accept the responsibilities of the office but that both he and Abū 'Ubaydah had refused.

The closing paragraph of the foregoing report is of special significance, and it runs as follows:

> ('Umar) said: "The voices rose louder and the clamor became much. And when I feared discord I said to Abū Bakr, 'Stretch your hand and I'll give you the *bay'ah.*' He did and I gave him my *bay'ah;* and so did the Muhājirūn and the Anṣār. Then we trampled on Sa'd (the Anṣārī candidate for caliph), and one of the Anṣār said, 'You killed Sa'd b. 'Ubādah.' I said, 'God killed him'. We, by God, could never have done better than to give the *bay'ah* to Abū Bakr. We feared to leave the place without concluding the *bay'ah*, for the Anṣār might proclaim someone else in our absence. If that had happened, we would have had to follow them in what we disliked or

[28] Ṭab., I, 1820-23; Athir, II, 326-28.

dispute them and cause wrong doing."[29]

These isolated references to 'Umar's reluctance to support Abū Bakr for the caliphate at first seem negligible in comparison with the large number of traditions emphasizing harmony between the two men who became successive caliphs. But, corroborated with the foregoing compilation of episodes where 'Umar opposed the prophet and his successor, these references seem to be more reliable and authentic than the studiously edited reports, where disputes among the early companions were systematically smothered. Most likely, what impelled 'Umar to yield to Abū Bakr's selection as the prophet's political successor was only the fear of discord and civil strife—and *not* that he really believed that nobody enjoyed the advantage of Abū Bakr's position. It is evident that a long time elapsed before the *bay'ah* to the first caliph and his control over the state's affairs were consolidated. The mere clap of his hand by 'Umar, as traditionists claim, was a gesture altogether insufficient to establish firmly the caliph's rule over the dissention-plagued Muslim community in Medina. It is also doubtful that 'Umar gave the *bay'ah* to Abū Bakr before it had become absolutely clear to him that he could not wrest the position for himself or for his closest associate, Abū 'Ubaydah.

ABU BAKR'S SUPPORT

If 'Alī and his group of the prophet's kinsmen withheld their *bay'ah* from Abū Bakr and claimed the legitimate right of 'Alī to the position of caliph, 'Umar and his group leaned towards the election of Abū 'Ubaydah, and the Anṣār strived to have a member of their own fill the vacancy; who, then,

[29] Ṭab., I, 1823. There seems to be an error in Ṭabarī's version; the article *lā* is omitted in the last line, while it is mentioned in Ibn al-Athīr's. See Athīr, II, 328. This story is given with some variations in Balādhurī's *Ansāb*, I, 583-84.

were the supporters of Abū Bakr? The vast majority of the traditional sources present Abū Sufyān as having been against the proclamation of Abū Bakr as caliph.[30] Also, Khālid b. Sa'īd, a prominent Umayyad and one of the earliest followers of Muḥammad, is reported to have been against the *bay'ah* to Abū Bakr.[31] These reports concerning two of the most prominent Umayyad chiefs originated in the works of well-known anti-Umayyad authors;[32] and yet it is difficult to disprove them because of the lack of counter pro-Umayyad traditions in the extant historical works. But, even granting the authenticity of these reports and that the Umayyads were actually against the election of Abū Bakr and for that of 'Alī—what about the rest of the Meccan aristocracy?

Khālid b. al-Walīd, for one, supported Abū Bakr. In a passage from *Kitāb al-muwaffaqīyāt* of al-Zubayr b. Bakkār, preserved in *Sharḥ nahj al-balāghah* of Ibn Abī al-Ḥadīd, the following is said about Khālid b. al-Walīd: "And Khālid was a *shī'ah* (supporter) of Abū Bakr and was among those who turned away from 'Alī." The reporter proceeds to give a speech, delivered by Khālid in support of Abū Bakr, in which he summed up the Meccan attitude toward Islam, past and present:

> We today are more than yesterday, and yesterday we were better than we are today. He who joins this religion, his reward will be in accordance with his deeds; and he who falls back from it, we will bring him back to it. And, by God, the holder of this affair [i.e., Abū Bakr] is not a man about whom one needs enquire, and his character needs not be sounded out."[33]

The same source, on the same authority, gives a long passage concerning the reaction of 'Amr b. al-'Aṣ, who was later to

[30] Ya'qūbī, II, 126; Bal. *Ans.*, I, 588-9; Ṭab., I, 1827; Athīr, II, 325-26.
[31] Ya'qūbī, II, 126; Bal. *Ans.*, I, 588; Ṭab., I, 2079-80.
[32] Isḥāq, Madā'inī, Wāqidī.
[33] Ibn Abī al-Ḥadīd, VI, 22.

become one of Abū Bakr's generals, to the affairs of the *saqīfah*. Quotations from that passage follow: 'Amr said: "[The Anṣār] are not equal to the Muhājirūn; Sa'd [b. 'Ubādah, the Anṣārī candidate for caliph] is not equal to Abū Bakr, and Medina is not equal to Mecca. [The Anṣār] fought us [Meccans] in the past and achieved supremacy over us at the beginning; but if we fight them today, we will achieve supremacy over them in the end." This speech reached the Anṣār and their speaker retorted in the same tone. When news of 'Amr's speech reached 'Alī, 'Alī cursed him furiously saying: "['Amr] has done wrong to God and His prophet." 'Alī then went to the mosque and delivered, in the presence of many Qurayshites, a long speech in praise of the Anṣār, at the end of which he said: "He who loves God and His prophet loves the Anṣār; let 'Amr curb himself from doing us wrong". Even so, the same pro-Meccan attitude as that of Khālid and 'Amr was taken, according to the foregoing source, by al-Walīd b. 'Uqbah, a prominent Umayyad:

> al-Zubayr [b. Bakkār] said: "Then al-Walīd b. 'Uqbah b. Abī Mu'ayṭ, who hated the Anṣār because they took his father captive in the battle of Badr and cut off his head in the presence of the prophet, stood up, abused the Anṣār, and spoke of them in obscene language." Dirār b. al-Khaṭṭāb, a Meccan chief and poet, Zayd b. al-Khaṭṭāb, brother of 'Umar, and Yazid b. Abī Sufyān blamed al-Walīd for vilifying the Anṣār.[35]

In another passage from the same source, the following is said:

> When Abū Bakr was given the *bay'ah* and his situation was stabilized, many among the Anṣār regretted that they had given him the *bay'ah*. They mentioned 'Alī b. Abī Ṭālib and cried out in his name. He, however, remained

[34]Ibn Abī al-Ḥadīd, VI, 29-34.
[35]Ibn Abī al-Ḥadīd, VI, 36-37.

> in his house and did not come out [in response] to their call. The Muhājirūn became concerned and much was said about that. The harshest on the Anṣār were the Qurayshites Suhayl b. 'Amr, a member of Banū 'Amir Lu'ayy, al-Ḥārith b. Hishām and 'Ikrimah b. Abī Jahl, from the clan of Makhzūm. These were the notables of Quraysh who had fought the prophet and who later adopted Islam. They all were wronged by the Anṣār, who had killed some of their relatives—and the blood revenge for whom was still denied.[36]

The foregoing quotations demonstrate clearly that the newly-converted Meccan aristocracy were the back-bone of Abū Bakr's group of supporters. This contention is confirmed by further circumstantial evidence revealed in a scrutiny of the background of those who collaborated with Abū Bakr in carrying out his policy. An examination of the list of leaders' names—to whom Abū Bakr entrusted the task of commanding the Muslim armies who conquered Arabia—shows the extent to which the first caliph drew on the Meccan aristocracy for implementation of his plans. Among these leaders one finds:

1) Khālid b. al-Walīd, from the clan of Makhzūm of Quraysh; a prominent leader in Mecca before Islam. He was in command of the Quraysh cavalry in all the battles between the Muslims and Meccans before al-Ḥudaybiyah. He adopted Islam only in the year 7.[37]

2) 'Amr b. al-'Aṣ, from the clan of Sahm of Quraysh. He adopted Islam together with Khālid shortly before the conquest of Mecca.[38]

3) 'Ikrimah b. Abī Jahl, from the clan of Makhzūm of Quraysh. He was the son of Abū Jahl, head of Makhzūm, who was killed in Badr. 'Ikrimah was as hostile to Islam and the prophet as his father had been, and he adopted Islam only

[36]Ibn Abī al-Ḥadīd, VI, 23.
[37]Ibn Ḥajar, *Iṣābah*, I, 412-13.
[38]Ibn Ḥajar, *Iṣābah*, III, 2.

after Mecca was conquered.[39]

4) al-'Alā' b. al-Ḥaḍramī, a client of the Umayyads of Quraysh.[40]

5) al-Muhājir b. Abī Umayyah, from the clan of Makhzūm of Quraysh. He was the brother of Umm Salamah, a wife of the prophet. He adopted Islam after Badr.[41]

6) Khālid b. Sa'īd b. al-'Aṣ, a prominent leader from the clan of Umayyah of Quraysh. He was among the first few who had adopted Islam.[42]

7) Yazid b. Abī Sufyān, son of the famous Abū Sufyān, leader of the Umayyad clan of Quraysh. He adopted Islam after the conquest of Mecca together with his father and his famous brother Mu'āwiyah.[43]

On the other hand, during the whole war in Arabia under Abū Bakr, names of people who had previously undertaken military commands, under the prophet, and who later were to assume leadership of conquest armies under 'Umar, are not recorded as having played a role in Abū Bakr's wars. This group of early Muhājirūn, opposed to Abū Bakr's policy of waging war against the tribes in Arabia and who saw in the Meccan aristocracy a threat to their position of prominence in the Muslim community, includes such people as:

1) Abū 'Ubaydah b. al-Jarrāḥ, from the clan of Fihr of Quraysh. He was one of the first ten who adopted Islam. During the lifetime of the prophet, he led a reinforcement to 'Amr b. al-'Aṣ, in the campaign of Dhāt al-Salāsil.[44] Under 'Umar, Abū 'Ubaydah replaced Khālid b. al-Walīd as commander of the Muslim armies in Syria.[45]

2) Sa'd b. Abī Waqqāṣ, from the clan of Zuhrah of

[39] *Ibid.*, II, 489.
[40] *Ibid.*, II, 491.
[41] *Ibid.*, III, 445.
[42] *Ibid.*, I, 406.
[43] *Ibid.*, III, 619.
[44] Dhahabī, *Siyar*, I, 5.
[45] *Ibid.*, I, 13.

Quraysh, one of the first ten to adopt Islam and later one of the six-member Shūrā (consultative council) whom 'Umar appointed for the purpose of selecting one from among their number to succeed him as caliph.[46] The prophet had sent him on a raid on Rābigh (in Ḥijāz).[47] Under 'Umar, Sa'd commanded the Muslim army that conquered Iraq.[48]

3) Abū 'Ubayd al-Thaqafī, who was appointed by 'Umar commander of an army that was dispatched to join the tribe of Shaybān in attacking Iraq.[49]

4) al-Zubayr b. al-'Awwām, from the clan of 'Abd al-'Uzzā of Quraysh. He was also one of the first then to adopt Islam and was a member of the Shūrā. The prophet had appointed him commander of part of the army that conquered Mecca.[50] Under 'Umar, al-Zubayr was dispatched to Egypt as a reinforcement to 'Amr b. al-'Aṣ.[51]

5) Others like 'Alī b. Abī Tālib, Ṭalḥah b. 'Abd Allah, 'Abd al-Raḥmān b. 'Awf—all of them early, prominent Muhājirūn and members of the Shūrā—did not play any role in the war under Abū Bakr.

The non participation of the prominent early Muhājirūn in the war under Abū Bakr, while they had fought and undertaken command under the prophet and 'Umar, does not seem to be a coincidence. Also, the selection by Abū Bakr of his army commanders mainly from Meccan aristocracy does not appear a haphazard result of chance. The Muhājirūn and Anṣār, each considering themselves more entitled to determining state policy than the new-comers, were antagonistic to the Meccans and had a common cause in preventing them from dominating the scene in Medina. Yet, because each group was claiming the right to succession for themselves on

[46] *Ibid.*, , I, 62.
[47] *Ibid.*, I, 67.
[48] *Ibid.*, I, 77.
[49] al-Dinawarī (Abū Ḥanīfah), *al-Akhbār al-Ṭiwāl*, 113.
[50] Dhahabī, *Siyar*, I, 33.
[51] *Ibid.*, I, 35.

the basis of services rendered to Islam in its infancy, these two groups were suspicious of each other and could not reach agreement between themselves against the Meccans. On the other hand, having just fought Islam with all its might, lost the battle, and surrendered to the prophet—the Meccan aristocracy was not able, in such a short period within the fold, to wrest the caliphate for any one of its own members. Under the prevailing circumstances, the Meccans sought to achieve the best they could in their own interest. From among the eligible candidates for caliph, Abū Bakr was best suited to that interest. Abū Bakr had always been a close associate of the prophet and promised to be an unwavering supporter of the master's unfinished political and military advances. Having exhibited a tendency to follow the prophet's favoritist policy toward the Meccans, Abū Bakr garnered their trust and support for his election to the caliphate and, in turn, rewarded them for that support by appointing them to the high positions of command.

* * *

If it is misleading to view the contending groups in Medina in terms of political parties with platforms and candidates, it would be just as misleading to view Abū Bakr's winning of the *bay'ah* as the result solely of Meccan support. The venerable old man enjoyed a position in the community which nobody else did. His relation to the prophet, his close association with the master, his mild character, and his devotion to the cause of Islam made him—as far as each of the contending groups was concerned—the second-best choice. When stalemate between the various groups was apparent and each group had failed to wrest the *bay'ah* for its own candidate without causing bloodshed, Abū Bakr was the only alternative acceptable to them all. He was acceptable to the early Muhājirūn because he was after all one of their members; he was accepted by the Meccans for his policy towards them;

and he was agreeable to the Anṣār because of his association with the prophet and his devotion to Islam. But the proclamation of Abū Bakr as caliph was still, in more ways than one, a victory for the Meccans. They were saved from the animosity of the Anṣār and the heavy hand of 'Umar. They secured, with the new caliph's favor, means to considerable gain for themselves. In appreciation of their support, Abū Bakr entrusted them with the command of the Muslim armies of the conquest.

Even though Abū Bakr's prestige contributed much to his securing the caliphal post, by itself, it was certainly insufficient to allow him to wage war as he did, against all those who did not yield to his authority, throughout Arabia. The Meccan merchants were not renowned for their warlike qualities; and, without a militant ally, they would never have been able to wage effective war. The tribes of the Ḥijāz, who were dependent on Quraysh for their livelihood, and those tribes on the trade routes, with whom Mecca had friendly relations, filled the gap. For a long time before Muḥammad, Quraysh had maintained good relations with these tribes and had concluded with them commercial pacts, known as *īlāf*.[52] From among these tribes, as will be discussed below, the Muslim commanders recruited their armies for the war in Arabia. The tribes in the Ḥijāz were certainly a tremendous pressure group in Medinan politics; and the Meccans, undoubtedly, relied on these tribes' support in challenging the Anṣār. Before the Meccans surrendered to Islam, the Ḥijāzī tribes had sent contingents to help the Meccans fight the Muslims in the battles of Uḥud and al-Khandaq;[53] and when Mecca gave in to Muḥammad, these tribes followed suit. Meccan influence was, undoubtedly, instrumental in keeping the tribes of

[52]For the *īlāf*, cf. M. Hamīdullah, "Al-īlāf, ou Les Rapports Economico-Diplomatiques de la Mecque pré-Islamique," *Mélange L. Massignon*, II, 293-311; M. J. Kister, "Mecca and Tamīm," *Journal of the Economic and Social History of the Orient*, VIII, P. II, Nov. 1965, 113-163.

[53]Watt, 30, 36.

Ḥijāz from turning against Medina after the death of the prophet. Tribal support enhanced the position of the Meccans in Medinan affairs and encouraged them to wage war against other tribes in Arabia. Abū Bakr relied on two forces, Meccans and their tribal allies, in bringing to fruition Muḥammad's aspirations. Furthermore, Abū Bakr was committed as caliph to waging those wars, committed to the fronts which had hoisted him into his new position of power.

THE ELECTION'S IMMEDIATE CONSEQUENCES

The question to ask at the outset here is whether, indeed, there was a policy for Abū Bakr to bring to fruition.

Muḥammad's policy of expansion to the north, the problems involved in the implementation of such a policy, and the impediments which hindered Muḥammad from carrying out his plans have already been mentioned. The possibility that the Meccans were the initiators of the policy as adopted by the prophet has been hinted. It was in Abū Bakr's time, however, that the existence of such an ambitious policy became obvious. No sooner had the caliph established his rule in Medina than he began dispatching his armies in different directions throughout Arabia. The Arab tribes in the Syrian Desert were not excluded from the plan of spreading Medina's hegemony over all Arabs, regardless of the sphere of influence under which they therefore had lived. Two Muslim commanders were sent to Syria at the same time that others were dispatched to different destinations within Arabia itself.[54]

The causes and nature of the Arab conquest have been studied by many historians in modern times, and many theories have been posited for the explanation of the phenomenon.[55] No new theory is advanced here; it is only a con-

[54]Cf. Chapter IV.

[55]Cf. G. H. Bousquet, "Quelques remarques critiques et sociologiques sur la conquête arabe et les théories émises à ce sujet," *Studi orientalistici in onore di Giorgio Levi Della Vida*, Pt. I, 52-60; *idem.*, "Observations sur la nature et les causes de la conquête arabe," *Studia Islamica*, 6 (1956), 37-52.

tention that both the prophet and his successor adopted a policy of expansion and that they worked out a plan for the implementation of that policy. Part of the plan was the conquest of Arabia. The war in the peninsula and the subsequent invasion of Syria were not chance episodes in the history of Islam. The prophet attempted to invade Syria and failed in his effort. The failure of the campaign to Tabūk caused him to change his policy towards the tribes of Arabia. His realization that an invasion of Syria would be impossible as long as the major part of Arabia was outside his control seems to have been what prompted him to amend that policy. Abū Bakr, following in Muḥammad's footsteps, undertook what was necessary to put that policy to work.

If for Muḥammad at the apex of his power the invasion of Syria proved to be far beyond what he could afford, for Abū Bakr it was even more so. When the prophet led the campaign to Tabūk in the year 9, he recruited all the forces he had at his disposal; and yet at Tabūk he realized that it would be suicidal, as Mu'tah had been before, to invade Syria. So, he returned to Medina, determined to subjugate all of Arabia to his rule before embarking on the Syrian adventure. The conquest of Arabia, as the preliminary step to the invasion of Syria, became even more urgent for Abū Bakr—if he too was to adopt the prophet's expansionist policy. As the caliph of Islam in dissention-stricken Medina, with a sizeable number of nomadic tribes breaking away from him, Abū Bakr had by far fewer forces at his disposal than Muḥammad had had. Abū Bakr had to choose between renouncing the policy of expansion, at least for the time being, and taking vigorous measures for its implementation. He—no doubt, with his supporters' blessings—chose the second alternative.

Whatever were the motives for expansion, it is evident that Abū Bakr's ultimate goal was to invade Syria. Whether he visualized an encounter with the two empires or not is a matter of conjecture; but, that the Arabs in the Syrian Desert were not excluded from his expansionist plan is quite evident.

He had, under adverse circumstances in Medina and its surroundings, made haste to send Usāmah on a campaign to the Syrian borders. While engaged in fighting in Arabia itself, the first caliph of Islam did not neglect the Syrian front: two distinguished commanders, ʿAmr b. al-ʿAṣ and Khālid b. Saʿīd, were later also dispatched to the Syrian border. As soon as Arabia was subjugated, tribes were recruited and sent to the Syrian front. The importance of the Syrian front to the Muslims is demonstrated by the fact that Khālid b. al-Walīd was ordered to leave the Iraqī front and hurry to help the Muslims in Syria, and not the other way around.[56]

The endeavor made by both the prophet and, following him, Abū Bakr to keep a foothold on the Syrian border, while their main military activities were diverted to Arabia after the campaign of Tabūk, indicate that the ultimate goal of that expansionist policy was control in Syria. The conquest of Arabia was the necessary first step in that direction, and it was mainly for the purpose of recruiting armies for the invasion of Syria.

This policy of expansion to the north seems to have been promoted, both during the prophet's lifetime and during that of Abū Bakr, by the Meccans. It is interesting to note that this line of policy was not accentuated until after the Meccans joined the Muslim state. It is most likely that the prospective material gains, which could be obtained through the success of such a policy, was what induced the Meccans formally to adhere to Islam.[57] If so, then there was little cause for them to forego this interest when Muḥammad died; on the contrary, they had every reason, still, for following it through. Inside the fold of Islam, the Meccans had been treated with deference by the prophet, and they found in him an inclination to listen to them. What they also found was an ally in the bedouins,

[56]De Goeje, *op. cit.*, 1.

[57]H. A. R. Gibb, "An interpretation of Islamic History," *Studies on the Civilization of Islam*, 5.

who like them, accepted Islam out of material interest and were enthusiastically willing to lend them a hand in promoting their cause. The tribesmen and the Meccans were the two principal elements in the first victories of Islam.[58] Both, as Mr. Gibb has so aptly put it, had a keen interest in expansion; the bedouins with their natural instinct for booty and for the appropriation of land for pasture and the Meccan merchants for the exploitation of that land to their commercial profit.[59]

While the tribesmen, being interested in pasture regardless of location, had no specific reason for the preference of Syria over any other region; the Meccans, being interested in trade, had a definite objective in that country—trade routes. During the sixth century, Mecca had emerged as the main metropolis of western Arabia by virtue of its becoming the hub of three trade routes. The first connected it with East Africa, the second with Baḥrayn through Yamāmah, and the third with Yemen. During the 6th century, because of the heavy duties imposed by both Byzantines and Persians on the commercial traffic which passed through the eastern route (Persian Gulf-Mesopotamia), the bulk of the trade with the East was diverted to the western routes, in Arabia, and fell into the hands of the Meccans.[60] The latter carried that trade to Syria and Palestine by way of the old spice-route. The eastern Mesopotamian route—which ran through territory inhabited by Arab tribes in the Syrian Desert and which was under strict supervision by the two empires—remained a strong potential competitor to the Meccans' spice route. It would seem the Meccans were anxious to lay their hands on the Syrian route and control that one, too.

Furthermore, eight years of struggle between Muḥammad and the Meccans, during which time the former's target was the latter's trade, had undoubtedly a dire effect on Meccan

[58] *Ibid.*, 6.

[59] *Ibid.*, 6.

[60] Irfan Kawar, "The Arabs in the Peace Treaty of A.D. 561," *Arabica* 3 (1956), 184-192.

trade. The Muslim raids on Meccan caravans before al-Ḥudaybiyah (and subsequent attacks by would-be Muslims[61] after the peace treaty) had certainly disrupted the Meccan trade on the spice-route. Meccan trade on the route from the east (from Baḥrayn) also had been blocked, first by Muslim raids on the caravans[62] and later through interception of that trade by the Muslim's allies. This route, which started in Baḥrayn and 'Uman and led to Mecca, was easily blocked by Banū Ḥanīfah, who inhabited al-Yamāmah. Before Mecca's surrender to Islam, Thumāmah b. Uthāl, a chief from Banū Ḥanīfah who became Muslim, is reported by the tradition to have obstructed Mecca's trade with al-Yamāmah.[63] After the conquest of Mecca and the beginning of hostilities with Banū Ḥanīfah under Musaylimah, Meccan trade on this route could not have been possible. If trade on this route was disrupted, there could have been only one other alternative for it: it would have to be diverted to the Mesopotamian route. And if the Meccans lost their trade, as they actually did,[64] then the Arab tribes in the Syrian Desert would have been the beneficiaries of the Meccan loss. In this case, with the Eastern trade falling into the hands of the Arabs who inhabited the areas around the Mesopotamian route, Meccan promotion of a policy of expansion towards Syria is most understandable; and their staunch support of Abū Bakr, who stood for such a policy, is readily explicable.

[61]Watt, 61.

[62]Watt, 5.

[63]Ibn Ḥanbal, *Musnad*, XIII, 92 (A. M. Shākir, ed.); Ibn Ḥajar, *Iṣābah*, I, 204.

[64]Watt, 59.

3. THE CHARACTER AND EXTENT OF THE RIDDAH

CONCERNING THE CHARACTER and extent of the so-called *Riddah,* there is as much disagreement in the sources as among modern historians. The word is usually applied to a movement among the Arab tribes after the death of the prophet to renounce whatever obligations they had previously had to Medina. The suppression of this movement and the invasion of Syria are the two major events of Abū Bakr's caliphate. Chroniclers as well as historians have paid very little attention to considerations beyond these two events in the two years of Abū Bakr's rule. Actually, after the first few days of his rule, in which he had to contend with the opposition in Medina, even Abū Bakr is up-staged by the glorious exploits of Khālid b. al-Walīd. Khālid, the hero of the Riddah, the chief general of Abū Bakr, the "Sword of God" as the prophet called him—from the day he was entrusted with the command of Muslim troops until the day he was deposed by 'Umar—attracts the central attention of traditionists, at least of those whose works are extant.

In this chapter, the events called by the general term of *al-Riddah* will be explored in detail in hopes of determining more accurately their true nature.

* * *

In the traditional accounts concerning the Riddah, the underlying assumption is that it was a religious movement directed against Islam and that the death of the prophet signalized the beginning of the tribes' break with Islam, their change of belief, and their revolt against the authority of Medina. For the traditionists, the leaders of the movement against Medina were "false prophets" who propagated a religion far inferior to that of Muḥammad.[1]

This additional Muslim assumption did not pass unchallenged by modern historians. But, with regard to this question, there is also a diversity of opinions among them. Following are a few representative examples.

The first to challenge the traditional view in the West was J. Wellhausen, who in his *Skizzen und Vorarbeiten*, asserts that the Riddah was a break with the leadership in Medina and not with Islam *qua* religion. Wellhausen proceeds to say that the prophets that arose in Arabia, like Muḥammad, called for the worship of Allah, not for the worship of other gods. The majority of the tribes wanted to continue worshipping Allah, but without having to pay any tax. In addition, the tribes' animosity was directed against agents of Islam, not its God or religion. But Wellhausen concedes that the death of Muḥammad signalized the beginning of the secession. The rebels were encouraged first by the strife within Medina itself over the succession to the prophet's position; then they took advantage of the fact that Medina was stripped of all its fighting force—sent under Usāmah to Syria—and they declared their secession.[2]

Caetani, consistent with his division of Arabia's tribes into groups according to their relations with the Muslim state in Medina, admits that the death of the prophet caused a great

[1]*E. I.*, article "Abū Bakr," W.M. Watt; Muir, *op. cit.*, 334; Dūrī, *op. cit.*, 42; Caetani, *Studi*, III, 354-358.

[2]Julius Wellhausen, *Skizzen und Vorarbeiten*, Berlin, 1884-99, Vol. VI, 7-8.

deal of commotion in Quraysh and possibly in Ṭā'if. But, according to him, Muḥammad's death caused actual breakaway from Medina only among the tribes of the second and third groups (viz. Ch. I). According to Caetani, these two groups regarded their "Islam" as an agreement with Muḥammad personally. They considered the election of Abū Bakr a private affair in Medina; they had not taken part in it and so did not feel themselves bound by it. These tribes wanted to negotiate a new agreement with Abū Bakr, but he refused to negotiate and insisted on exacting in full the agreements they had made with the prophet. Caetani concludes that the Riddah was not an apostasy and that these wars were based on political matters. He concedes that only Wellhausen before him reached, correctly, this conclusion.[3]

A concise résumé of the history of the Riddah, availing itself of the research of both Wellhausen and Caetani on the subject, is given by Becker. Here are the main points of Becker's views: 1) It was inexplicable to early historians that so many wars were necessary for the subjugation of Arabia to Islam after the death of Muḥammad, and they accounted for them by Riddah, general apostasy. 2) The death of Muḥammad was doubtless reason enough to secede for all those who had followed him unwillingly. 3) The majority of those regarded as secessionists had never adopted Islam before. 4) Prophetism gained ground in Arabia in imitation of Muḥammad. 5) The fight against the Riddah was not a fight against apostates; the tribes' objections were to the supremacy of Medina and to taxes rather than to Islam as such. 6) Only a few tribes accepted the leadership of Abū Bakr, the others seceded. 7) With Medina denuded of its army after the departure of Usāmah, some former allies wished to exploit Medina's precarious position by staging a sudden attack. 8) Abū Bakr with great energy fought the secessionists.[4]

[3] Caetani, *Studi*, III, 349-52.
[4] Becker, *op. cit.*, 335-36.

Bernard Lewis sums up the problem of the Riddah as he sees it, saying:

> The first task of the new regime was to counter by military action a movement among the tribes known to the tradition as the *Riddah*. This word, which means apostasy, in fact represents a distortion of the real significance of events by the theologically coloured outlook of later historians. The refusal of the tribes to recognize the succession of Abū Bakr was in effect not a relapse by converted Muslims to their previous paganism, but the simple and automatic termination of a political contract by the death of one of the parties. The tribes nearest to Medina had in fact been converted and their interests were so closely identified with those of the Umma that their separate history has not been recorded. For the rest the death of Muḥammad automatically severed their bonds with Medina, and the parties resumed their liberty of action. They felt in no way bound by the election of Abū Bakr in which they had taken no part, and at once suspended both tribute and treaty relations. In order to re-establish the hegemony of Medina, Abū Bakr had to make new treaties. While some of the nearer tribes accepted these, the more distant ones refused, and Abū Bakr was compelled to undertake the military subjugation of these tribes as a prelude to their conversion.[5]

In contradistinction to the foregoing scholars, Watt is much more receptive to the Muslim historians' point of view. For him

> there is nothing surprising or impossible in a mass movement into the Islamic community in the ninth and tenth years of the Hijrah, and consequently there is no justification for rejecting outright the statements in the sources because they tend to glorify Muḥammad. It may, in

[5]Lewis, 51-52.

European analytical terms, be primarily a political movement, but in the integral reality of the events, the religious and political factors were inseparable. To this movement the Riddah was a reaction. It was not the mere revival of anything old, whether paganism or pro-Byzantine or pro-Persian Christianity. It doubtless had roots in these religious systems, but the reaction of pagan or Christian Arabs to the circumstances created by the growth of the Islamic community produced something new. Moreover, as in the movement towards Islam, so in the Riddah, religious and political factors were inseparably mixed with one another. The Muslim historians were therefore right in regarding it as a religious movement; it was European scholars who erred by taking 'religion' in a European and not an Arab sense. The Riddah was a movement away from the religious, social, economic, and political system of Islam, and so was anti-Islamic.

Although the tradition asserts that most of the leaders of the Riddah made their appearance as prophets and, naturally, calls them false—still, very little can be learned from the sources about the religious teachings of those prophets. There is almost nothing that could be added to what historians have said about the religious aspects of the movement headed by these prophets.[7] Watt has put it as follows:

> In al-Bahrayn and 'Umān there seems to have been little mention of religion; but elsewhere the special feature of the Riddah was the appearance of "false prophets," each preaching a new religion with himself as centre. Our sources are too meagre for us to be certain about the background of these prophets, how far inspired by Islam and how far a similar but independent reaction to similar

[6]Watt, 147-48.

[7]*E. I.*, articles "Ṭulaiḥah" by V. Vacca; "Sadjāḥ" by V. Vacca; "Musailima" by Fr. Buhl; "al-Aswad al-'Ansī" by W. M. Watt; Caetani, *Studi*, III, 354-58, 374-77.

circumstances. We do not know whether their supporters were mainly nomads or mainly agriculturists. If the supporters were settled, then the movements might be responses to the challenge from which Islam arose—the change from a nomadic to a settled economy; if the supporters were nomads, the challenge might be the destructive effect of constant feuds. The impression given is that only Musaylimah was trying to deal with social and economic problems of his locality; but this may be due to lack of evidence about the others.[8]

* * *

What was this movement called Riddah? How wide-spread was it? These are the main questions around which the discussion will evolve in this chapter. A practical way to deal with these questions is to survey the reports in the traditional sources, collate them and try to draw some conclusions that might serve to answer these questions.

During the year 10 A.H. the prophet is reported to have sent his agents to those tribes who adopted Islam to collect the tax.[9] Ibn Isḥāq gives the following report:

> The prophet had sent his emirs and agents to all the places in which Islam prevailed to collect the tax. He sent al-Muhājir b. Abī Umayyah to Ṣan'ā', there al-'Ansī rose against him. He also sent Ziyād b. Labīb al-Bayādī, of the Anṣār, to Ḥaḍramawt; 'Adīy b. Ḥātim to Tayyi' and Asad; and Mālik b. Nuwayrah al-Yarbū'ī to Banū Ḥazalah to collect the tax. He divided the task of collecting the tax from Banū Sa'd between two members of the tribe: al-Zibirqān b. Badr was in charge of one part and 'Asim b. Qays of the other. He also had sent

[8]Watt, 148.

[9]Isḥāq, 1018; Ṭabarī, I, 1750; Athīr, II, 301. This piece of information is transmitted on the authority of Ibn Isḥāq.

> al-ʿAlā b. al-Ḥaḍramī to Baḥrayn. And he sent ʿAlī b. Abī Ṭālib to the people of Najrān to collect the tax from them and come back to him [Muḥammad] with the tribute.[10]

If this report of Ibn Isḥāq—telling which among the tribes outside the Ḥijāz were supposed to pay the tax—can be confirmed and proven valid and if it can be determined which of these tribes actually did pay and which did not and why—then an answer can be established to a key problem concerning the character and extent of the Riddah.

The lists of names of the prophet's agents given elsewhere in the sources confirm the report of Ibn Isḥāq. They also include, however, the names of Muḥammad's agents among tribes in the Ḥijāz and Wādī al-Qurā whom ibn Isḥāq seems to have taken for granted.[11] Only the Christians of Najrān are reported to have paid the tax;[12] from the rest, Abū Bakr had to exact the tax that was due by force. But, the best evidence of the veracity of Ibn Isḥāq's report is in the various reports in the sources concerning the happenings in the different parts of Arabia immediately following Muḥammad's death.

In this chapter, as in Chapter one, the course of events will be related regionally rather than chronologically.

THE ḤIJAZ

It has already been stated that the tribes of the Ḥijāz joined the Muslim state and identified their interests with those of the state. The vast majority of the sources exclude the tribes of Mecca, Medina, and Ṭā'if from those apostatizing. There is, however, a report to the effect that the majority of the

[10]Isḥāq, 1018.

[11]Ibn Ḥabīb, 126; Ya'qūbi, II, 122; Bal. *Ans.*, I, 529-531; Ṭab., I, 1908-09; Diyārbakrī, II, 202.

[12]Isḥāq, 1021-22; Sa'd, II/I, 122; Bal. *Ans.*, I, 384; Athīr, II, 301.

inhabitants of Mecca were about to apostatize had it not been for Suhayl b. 'Amr.[13] The falsity of this report is attested to by the fact that no other source mentions any movement in either Mecca or Medina against Islam. On the contrary, most sources, although unclear and confused about other parts of Arabia, are definite and give decisive statements concerning the non-participation in the Riddah of the inhabitants of the two sanctuaries, Mecca and Medina.[14] As additional proof of this report's falsity stands the fact that the majority of the commanders of the Muslim army against the "backsliders" were leaders of Meccan clans.[15] Within the social framework of Arab tribes at the time, it is hard to visualize clans turning against their leaders. This report, about apostasy in Mecca, seems to be a later forgery to blacken the Meccans and their Umayyad governor; and the tradition, which is ascribed to the prophet about Suhayl b. 'Amr, if anything, is there to lend credence to the parallel report. The tradition foretells of a praiseworthy stand Suhayl will take with relation to Islam in a critical time.[16]

In the Ḥijāz, a general loyalty to the Muslim state was kept not only by the inhabitants of the three towns (Mecca, Medina, and Ṭā'if) but also by the nomadic tribes who followed this example. These tribes were economically and politically dependent on the three centers and were among the first converts to Islam. They responded with alacrity to Abū Bakr's call to send contingents to fight the "apostate" tribes.[17]

The question on which the inhabitants of the Ḥijāz differed and squabbled was not whether to support the Muslim state;

[13]Diyārbakrī, II, 201; this report is added to the *sīrah* of Ibn Isḥāq by Ibn Hishām on the authority of Abū 'Ubaydah. Cf. Ibn Isḥāq, 1079.

[14]Ṭab., I, 1871; al-'Aynī, *'Umdah* (*Kitāb al-Zakāt, bāb wujūb al-zakāt*), VIII, 243; Diyārbakrī, II, 201; Ibn Kathīr, VI, 312.

[15]Ṭab., I, 1880-81.

[16]Isḥāq, 1079; Diyārbakrī, II, 201.

[17]Ṭab., I, 1905, 1910, 1921; Athīr, II, 351; Diyārbakrī, II, 204; al-'Aynī, *'Umdah*, VIII, 245.

it was rather over the question of succession to Muḥammad's position. Yet, inspite of these problems, the Ḥijāz could draw on enough power to fight the "apostates" and eventually to master Arabia and set out on the conquest movement. In view of the situation in Medina after the death of the prophet, it seems that the Meccans and the nomadic tribes of the Ḥijaz played the most significant role in ensuing events. While Meccans and nomads seem to have worked in complete harmony, the antagonism of the Anṣār to Meccan leadership did not abate soon. More on this subject will be said later in the chapter.

NAJD

For reasons connected with the sequence of events in the Riddah, it is advisable to start with the groups of Ghaṭafān, Ṭayyi', and Asad, and to deal with them together. Next comes Tamīm, then Banū Ḥanīfah—where , in each, conditions differed extremely from conditions in the other groups.

I. *Ghaṭafān, Ṭayyi', and Asad*

According to the report of Ibn Isḥāq, 'Adīy b. Ḥātim, a chief of Ṭayyi', was delegated by the prophet to collect the taxes from his tribe and from Asad. It is evident that what is meant by "Asad" in this report is a minority within the tribe of Asad which was inimical to Ṭalḥah and leaned towards Muḥammad.[18] It is also evident that 'Adīy collected the tax only from his clan, a subdivision of Ṭayyi', since parts of the tribe were on Ṭalḥah's side during the Riddah, as will be shown.

There is no mention of the tribe of Ghaṭafān in the report of Ibn Isḥāq. However, al-Balādhurī, who on the whole confirms Ibn Isḥāq, does mention some groups of Ghaṭafān.[19]

[18]Cf. Chapter I.
[19]Bal. *Ans.*, I, 530.

Other sources confirm al-Balādhurī and mention some groups from Ghaṭafān as having withheld the tax.[20] It is most likely that those parts of Ghaṭafān which allied themselves with Medina were, like others, asked by the prophet to pay the tax.

It is interesting to note that neither Ibn Isḥāq nor the other sources mention Ṭalḥah as an agent of Medina to his tribe, Asad. While, according to Ibn Isḥāq, the chiefs of Ṭayyi' and Tamīm were appointed agents of Medina and each was entrusted with the task of collecting the tax from his own clan; a man from Ṭayyi'—'Adīy—was appointed to Asad. In view of the old hostility between the two tribes, Asad and Ṭayyi', and considering Muḥammad's behavior towards the rest of the tribes in the area, it seems peculiar that an outsider, especially one from the inimical Ṭayyi', was appointed to Asad as an agent. The appointment of 'Adīy could not have been to all of Asad. The absence of Ṭalḥah's name from the report of Ibn Isḥāq and the behavior of Asad under the leadership of Ṭalḥah during the Riddah help in interpreting Ibn Isḥāq's report.

None, in this group of tribes, however, is reported to have actually paid the tax to Muḥammad. 'Adīy is reported to have collected it; but before he sent it to Medina, the prophet died. His tribe pressed him to return what he had collected. He succeeded in calming them and convinced them to wait and see what might happen in Medina. When Abū Bakr was elected and had dispatched the Army of Usāmah, 'Adīy secretly sent the tax to Abū Bakr.[21] But, Fazārah and Sulaym, branches of Ghaṭafān, retrieved what they had paid and forced the agents of the prophet to flee.[22]

The sources speak of a delegation from these tribes to Medina to negotiate with Abū Bakr; they asked to be exemp-

[20] Diyārbakrī, II, 203.

[21] Diyārbakrī, II, 203; Ibn 'Abd al-Barr, 1057; Ibn Ḥajar, *Iṣābah*, II, 461.

[22] Diyārbakrī, II, 203; Ṭab., I, 1870.

ted from paying the tax and pledged to continue to perform the prayer. Abū Bakr refused their request.[23] It is evident that this is a later formulation of the issue by religiously oriented Muslim historians. These tribes had not become Muslim; and even if they had, it is difficult to imagine nomads performing the prayer five times a day. They do not today and it seems that they never did. This formulation was apparently coined to account for juristic arguments concerning apostasy. It seems more likely that the delegations negotiated a continuation of their alliance with Medina without payment. That the tax was the main issue is supported by the often-mentioned statement Abū Bakr made: "If they withhold a hobbling-cord from the tax I would fight them for it."[24] With Abū Bakr's insistance on procuring the tax, the tribes were left with no choice but to pay or to take to arms. This is what actually happened.

When the negotiations failed, the delegation returned home with the news. A few decided to abide by their agreement with the prophet, and they paid the tax to Abū Bakr.[25] The rest—from the three tribes, Ghaṭafān, Asad, and Ṭayyi'—started to prepare for war against Medina, concluded alliances among themselves, and rallied around Ṭalḥah b. Khuwaylid, the leader of Asad,[26] whom the tradition presents as a false prophet. These allied groups were defeated in the battle of Buzākhah, which is discussed further on.

II. Tamīm

Although Tamīm did not adopt Islam during the prophet's lifetime, it seems to have agreed to pay the tax to Medina.[27]

[23] Ṭab., I, 1870, 1874, 1894; Athīr, II, 344; al-'Aynī, '*Umdah*, VIII, 244; Diyārbakrī, II, 202.

[24] This quotation is found in practically every source about this period.

[25] Ṭab., I, 1877-78; Athīr, II, 345; Diyārbakrī, II, 203.

[26] Ya'qubī, II, 129; Bal. *Fut.*, I, 115; Ṭab., I, 1874, 1886, 1893; Athīr, II, 342, 344.

[27] Watt, 140.

The report of Ibn Isḥāq confirms this, and it names three chiefs of different Tamīmī clans as having been in charge of collecting the tax; the names given are Mālik b. Nuwayrah, al-Zibirqān b. Badr, and 'Aṣim b. Qays. Other reports mention that the prophet appointed seven chiefs to the task.[28] But, none of these chiefs is reported to have paid the tax to Muḥammad.

The death of the prophet and the ensuing squabble in Medina put the jealous leaders of Tamīm in a very uncomfortable position. The tribe was evidently unwilling to pay the tax, the chiefs were competing among themselves for prominence, and the situation in Medina was unpredictable. Were one chief to pay the tax to Abū Bakr and the situation in Medina to deteriorate, he would be discredited by his tribe—especially if others had not paid. And if he did not pay and Abū Bakr proved to be a worthy successor to Muḥammad, that chief would be discredited in Medina—especially if others had paid.[29]

At that point, while Tamīm was split into rival parties, the "false prophetess" Sajāḥ made her appearance in the tribe and deepened the cleavage among the parties.[30] Some chiefs allied themselves with Sajāḥ, others rose against her, the rest were hesitant to side with anyone.[31] But, except for Mālik b. Nuwayrah, the chiefs of Tamīm, one by one, sent the tax to Abū Bakr before the Muslim army entered their territory.[32] Mālik withheld the tax and did not follow the example of the

[28] Ṭab., I, 1908-09; Athīr, II, 353; it is possible to reconcile this report with that of Ibn Isḥāq. In Ṭabarī and in Ibn al-Athīr the report is the same and originates in Sayf b. 'Umar, who is known for his detailed reports.

[29] Ṭab., I, 1909-10; Athīr, II, 353-54. The report is on the authority of Sayf b. 'Umar, who was a Tamīmī himself.

[30] Ṭab., I, 1911; Athīr, II, 354.

[31] Ṭab., I, 1911-14.

[32] Ṭab., I, 1909, 1922; Athīr, II, 354; Ibn Ḥajar, *Iṣābah*, I, 525; II, 182; III, 336.

others even when the Muslim army came to him. He was captured and killed on the order of Khālid b. al-Walīd.[33]

Thus, what took place among the tribes of Ghaṭafān, Tayyi', Asad, and Tamīm, following the death of the prophet, confirms the report of Ibn Isḥāq. Indications that some tribes sent the tax to Abū Bakr, that others withheld it and sent a delegation to negotiate a new agreement with him, while others defied the new caliph and prepared for war, support the report of Ibn Isḥāq that the prophet, before his death, had sent agents to collect the tax from tribes in that area which had allied themselves with Medina.

III. Banū Hanīfah

No agreement as to alliance or paying of a tax was ever reached between Muḥammad and Banū Ḥanīfah, and the vast majority of the tribe supported Musaylimah during Musaylimah's lifetime. Ibn Isḥāq's report does not mention Banū Ḥanīfah among the tribes to whom Muḥammad sent his agents to collect the tax. This supports the conclusion arrived at in chapter one's discussion of the extent of Muḥammad's control over Banū Ḥanīfah, just as consequent events among this tribe, following the death of the prophet, confirm Ibn Isḥāq's report. The issues of which the tradition speaks concerning Banū Ḥanīfah are different from those of the other tribes in Najd. Here, the significant issue is not the tax; rather it is Muḥammad's prophethood and the hegemony of Medina over Arabia.[34] Musaylimah's claim that he was a prophet is in itself a denial of Muḥammad's prophethood, especially since Muḥammad claimed to be the "Seal of Prophets." The insistance of the leaders of Banū Ḥanīfah on sharing with Medina the rule over Arabia[35] blocked the

[33]Ṭab., I, 1925, 1928; Bal. *Fut.*, I, 117. This episode will be discussed in further detail later on.

[34]Ya'qūbī, II, 129; Bal. *Fut.*, I, 105-106; Ṭab., I 1748-49; Diyārbakrī, II, 157, 159.

[35]Bal. *Fut.*, I, 107; Ṭab., I, 1748-49; Diyārbakrī, II, 157.

prophet's and Abū Bakr's plans to unify the Arabs under Muslim rule.

The Banū Ḥanīfah were a strong tribe and were unified around Musaylimah.[36] The kind of jealousies that the sources speak of concerning Tamīm, Ghaṭafān, Ṭayyi', and Asad are not found in Banū Ḥanīfah. The small splinter of this tribe which was antagonistic to Musaylimah and which was led by Thumāmah b. Uthāl, who allied himself with Medina, was not of much significance. Those individuals who did not support Musaylimah were few and weak to the extent that they had to flee Yamāmah when Musaylimah started to prepare for the pending encounter with the Muslim army.[37] Banū Ḥanīfah, under the command of Musaylimah, fought the fiercest battle the Muslim army saw in Arabia.[38] Not like others in Najd who were willing to accept the hegemony of Medina provided they be exempted from the payment of a tax which was imposed on them. Banū Ḥanīfah were decided to keep their independence and fight any intruder on their territory. No question of tax is mentioned in their regard in the sources.

In contrast with others, the behavior of Banū Ḥanīfah confirms the report of Ibn Isḥāq that the tribe was not asked to pay the tax. This indicates that they were different from any other group in Najd; battles fought against them were not because they broke any agreement, revolted against the old master, or withheld a due tax. It was, rather, a war to bring them under the control of Medina for the first time. Traditional sources, nonetheless, include the battles with Banū Ḥanīfah as part of the Riddah.

[36] Bal. *Fut.*, I, 105; Ṭab., I, 1938; Athīr, II, 361; Diyārbakrī, II, 158.
[37] Ṭab., I, 1910; Wathīmah, 13, 17; Diyārbakrī, II, 159.
[38] Bal. *Fut.*, I, 106; Ṭab., I, 1942; Athīr, II, 363; Diyārbakrī, II, 213, 216-17.

THE COASTAL AREAS

I. Baḥrayn

The reports in the sources concerning the Riddah in Baḥrayn are fragmentary and do not constitute a complete story of what took place in that area after Muḥammad's death. These sources are confused as regards al-'Alā' b. al-Ḥaḍramī, whose name is frequently mentioned in relation with Baḥrayn, and who apparently had undertaken several missions to that area. According to the report of Ibn Isḥāq, al-'Alā' was sent by the prophet in the year 10 to collect the tax from Baḥrayn. In another report, the same authority presents a story to the effect that al-'Alā remained in Baḥrayn as the agent of the prophet, since he was sent to al-Mundhir b. Sāwā, "king" of Baḥrayn.[39] In this same report, Ibn Isḥāq mentions al-'Alā' as the commander of the Army sent by Abū Bakr to subdue the "apostates" in Baḥrayn. He does not, however, supply any information concerning what al-'Alā' did when the prophet died and the people of Baḥrayn "apostatized."

The sources are all agreed upon al-'Alā''s being the commander of the Muslim army which conquered Baḥrayn during the caliphate of Abū Bakr.[40] One might well question whether al-'Alā' was in Baḥrayn at the time of the prophet's death and whether he remained there or returned to Medina, and why. The sources are either vague or silent concerning these questions and furnish only bits and pieces of information on the background of the situation in Baḥrayn. But the scanty information available fits together to give a meaningful answer to these questions.

Without quoting his authorities, al-Balādhurī gives the following report:

> They said: the prophet discharched al-'Alā' and appoint-

[39]Ṭab., I, 1959.

[40]Bal. *Fut.*, I, 99; Ṭab., I, 1958, 1962; Athīr, II, 369.

> ed Abān b. Sa'īd b. al-'Āṣī b. Umayyah as agent in Baḥrayn; others say: al-'Alā' was on one side of Baḥrayn, which included Qaṭīf, and Abān was on the other, which included al-Khaṭṭ. The first version, however, is more reliable. [In the following report al-Balādhurī adds]: When the prophet died, Abān left Baḥrayn. The people in Baḥrayn then asked Abū Bakr to reappoint al-'Alā', and he did.[41]

Sayf b. 'Umar gives three reports which add some more information. The essential points in these reports are confirmed by other sources. In the first report Sayf tells that al-Mundhir b. Sāwā died shortly after the prophet.[42] In the second he adds that al-Mundhir was busy fighting the tribe of Rabī'ah in his last days. After his death his followers were besieged in two places until al-'Alā' came and rescued them.[43] The third supplies more information about the revolt of Rabī'ah against al-Mundhir b. Sāwā. According to this report, al-Ḥuṭam b. Dubay'ah (from Qays b. Tha'labah, from Bakr b. Wā'il, from Rabī'ah) revolted against al-Mundhir shortly after the death of the prophet. The supporters of al-Ḥuṭam were comprised of "apostates" from Rabī'ah and others who were still "infidels." He captured Qaṭīf and Hajar and attracted the people of al-Khaṭṭ to his side. He surrounded the tribe of 'Abd al-Qays, who was helping the Muslims. He wanted to install a descendant of the royal family of Ḥīrah as "king" in Baḥrayn. The Muslims suffered badly from the siege and sought help from Abū Bakr. The latter dispatched al-'Alā' to fight the "apostates" in Baḥrayn.[44]

From these reports, it seems that the prophet sent an agent, probably two, to Baḥrayn to collect the tax. This confirms the report of Ibn Isḥāq. In Baḥrayn, the agents of the prophet

[41] Bal. *Fut.*, I, 99.
[42] Ṭab., I, 1958; Ibn Ḥajar, *Iṣābah*, III, 439; cf. also, Bal. *Fut.*, I, 101.
[43] Ṭab., I, 1959; Athīr, II, 368.
[44] Ṭab., I, 1961; cf. also Ṭab., I, 1960; Bal. *Fut.*, I, 101; Athīr, II, 368.

were met with a rebellion of Rabī'ah against al-Mundhir b. Sāwā—the ally of Muḥammad. These agents apparently were forced to flee Baḥrayn and return to Medina in the face of the revolt. After Abū Bakr had established himself in Medina and dispatched the Muslim army to fight the tribes in Najd, the followers of al-Mundhir (who had apparently died in the meantime) sought the help of Abū Bakr. The latter dispatched al-'Alā', reportedly with Tamīmīs, to fight Rabī'ah and subdue Baḥrayn.[45]

In Baḥrayn, as in Yamāmah, the issues discussed in the sources are different from those in Najd; here the sources do not raise the question of the tax. It is evident that no tax was paid to the agents of Muḥammad at this point. The ally of Muḥammad, who was previously the agent of the Persians in Baḥrayn, had lost his authority over the tribes there and was in urgent need of outside help. It is evident also that the revolt in Baḥrayn was absolutely different from what took place in Najd or Yamāmah—yet, in spite of this obvious difference, the tradition included this moment in the Riddah.

II. 'Umān

In many ways, the situation in 'Umān resembled that in Baḥrayn at the time. Here also, the prophet supported the sons of the previous agent of the Persians. In the report of Ibn Isḥāq, no mention is made of 'Umān. Other sources, however, bring reports (some on the authority of Ibn Isḥāq himself) to the effect that 'Amr b. al-'Aṣ was an agent of the prophet in 'Umān. These sources are definite about 'Amr's being in 'Umān at the time of the prophet's death. They also are all agreed that he left 'Umān upon the arrival of the news about the death of the prophet.[46]

According to the tradition, the prophet sent 'Amr to 'Umān

[45]Ṭab., I, 1963 ff.

[46]Ibn Ḥabīb, 77; Bal. *Fut.*, I, 92; Ṭab., I, 1561- 1959-60; Sa'd, I/II, 18; Athīr, II, 352; Diyārbakrī, II, 183-208.

in the year 8.[47] Without quoting his authorities, al-Balādhurī says that the prophet ordered his agents to collect the tax from the rich and distribute it among the poor.[48] This, reportedly, was the case in Yemen also; the agents were ordered to distribute the tax among the poor.[49] These instances are often quoted as evidence for juristic matters concerning taxation, and beneficiaries of the tax. Actually, al-Balādhurī brings forth this information in a juristic context, which makes its historical reliability doubtful.

The source material concerning 'Umān at this juncture is scanty and fragmentary. But these pieces of information put together give a reasonably clear picture of what took place in 'Umān after the death of the prophet. All the traditional sources are agreed that Muḥammad sent 'Amr to the two sons of al-Julandā only.[50] Ibn Ḥabīb adds that when they adopted Islam, they achieved supremacy in 'Umān.[51] No contact is reported to have been made with Laqīt b. Mālik. The latter, however, is described by Sayf b. 'Umar as having been equal to al-Julandā before Islam.[52] Laqīt, known as "the Crowned" is reported to have apostatized after the death of the prophet and to have forced the two sons of al-Julandā, the allies of the Muslims, to seek refuge in the mountains.[53] It is noteworthy that—although, according to Sayf, Jayfar b. al-Julandā sought the help of Abū Bakr, who dispatched an army to 'Umān—Balādhurī does not mention that Jayfar sought the help of Abū Bakr.

These reports confirm Ibn Isḥāq's: no agent was sent to 'Umān in the year 10 simply because 'Amr had already been

[47]Cf. Chapter I.

[48]Bal. *Fut.*, I, 93. This report seems to have originated in al-Wāqidī; *viz.* Ibn Sa'd, I/II, 18; Athīr, II, 272.

[49]Bal. *Fut.*, I, 87.

[50]Chapter I.

[51]Ibn Ḥabīb, 77.

[52]Ṭab., I, 1977; Athīr, II, 372.

[53]Bal. *Fut.*, I, 92; Ṭab. I, 1977; Athīr, II, 372.

there. They also indicate clearly that the two sons of al-Julandā had lost the authority their father had commanded in 'Umān. It is also obvious from these reports that Laqīt and his group of supporters did not ally themselves with the Muslims. On the contrary, it is most likely they remained hostile and probably forced 'Amr to flee 'Umān when the prophet died. There is much resemblance between the movement of Laqīt in 'Umān and that of al-Ḥuṭam in Baḥrayn. But, in spite of its obvious difference from other movements in Arabia at that time, the revolt of Laqīt is traditionally included in accounts of the Riddah.

III. Yemen

The situation in Yemen at this juncture was different from that in any other area in Arabia. What with the rule of the Abnā' limited to Ṣan'ā', the large number of tribes dwelling in the area, and the lack of a leader of any stature to substitute for the Abnā': chaos prevailed in Yemen. Many tribes of Yemen had reportedly sent delegations to Medina and had supposedly adopted Islam.[55] The tradition presents a picture wherein the whole area to the south of Mecca turned Muslim in a very short time and the prophet appointed agents to the tribes as if they were all under his control.[56] This claim of the tradition is baseless as a scrutiny of the many reports concerning the happenings in Yemen around the time of the prophet's death shows. Many of these reports will be discussed and criticized below, but first a compilation of the major events, recorded in the tradition, would help to clarify the situation in Yemen.

It is reported that Yemen became Muslim and that the prophet recognized Bādhām, head of the Abnā', as his agent

[54]Ṭab., I, 1977; Athīr, II, 372.

[55]Cf. Chapter I.

[56]Sa'd, I/II, 59-86; Bal. *Fut.*, I, 82-91; Ṭab., I, 1851-1855; Athīr, II, 293-300.

over all Yemen.[57] After the death of Bādhām, Muḥammad appointed several agents over the different tribes of Yemen.[58] Al-Aswad rose against these agents and forced them to flee Yemen.[59] Qays b. Makshūḥ and ʿAmr b. Maʿdīkarib collaborated with al-Aswad; in Ṣanʿā' the Abnā' were among al-Aswad's entourage.[60] Qays and the Abnā' conspired against al-Aswad and murdered him.[61] After the death of al-Aswad, Abū Bakr appointed Fayrūz, a prominent leader of the Abnā' as agent over Ṣanʿā'.[62] Qayt then turned against the Abnā' and forced them out of Ṣanʿā'.[63] Abū Bakr sent an army under al-Muḥājir to subdue Qays.[64]

According to the report of Ibn Isḥāq the prophet sent al-Muḥājir b. Abī Umayyah to Ṣanʿā' and Ziyad b. Labīd to Ḥadramawt as agents in the year 10. He also sent ʿAlī b. Abī Ṭālib to Najrān to collect the alms from the Muslims and the tribute from the others. ʿAlī is the only one who is reported to have collected the tax and returned.[65] There is, however, disagreement concerning al-Muḥājir. The controversy turns on whether al-Muḥājir, Khālid b. Saʿīd, or Shehr b. Bādhām, from the Abnā, was the agent of the prophet in Ṣanʿā'.[66] Balādhurī and Ibn Ḥabīb report that Khālid was assigned to Ṣanʿā' while al-Muḥājir was assigned to Kindah and al-Ṣadif.[67] After the death of the prophet, Balādhurī adds,

[57]Bal. *Fut.*, I, 126; Ṭab., I, 1851.

[58]Bal. *Fut.*, I, 82-83; Ṭab., I, 1852-53.

[59]Bal. *Fut.*, I, 125-27; Ṭab., I, 1795, 1856, 1863, 1983; Athīr, II, 340; Diyārbakrī, II, 155.

[60]Bal. *Fut.*, I, 126; Ṭab., I, 1864-68; Athīr, II, 337-38; Bayhaqī, *Sunan*, VIII, 176; Diyārbakrī, II, 156.

[61]Bal. *Fut.*, I, 126; Ṭab., I, 1866-67; Athīr, II, 338.

[62]Ṭab., I, 1990.

[63]Bal. *Fut.*, I, 127; Ṭab., I, 1989-92; Athīr, II, 376.

[64]Bal. *Fut.*, I, 127; Ṭab., I, 1998; Athīr, II, 377.

[65]Isḥāq, 1021-22; Saʿd, II/I , 122; Bal. *Ans.*, I, 384; Athīr, II, 301.

[66]Bal. *Fut.*, I, 83, 120; Ibn Ḥabīb, 126; Bal. *Ans.*, I, 529; Ṭab., I, 1853; Maqrīzī, 31.

[67]Ibn Ḥabīb, 126; Bal. *Fut.*, I, 82; Bal. *Ans.*, I, 529; Maqrīzī, 31.

Abū Bakr annexed Kindah and al-Ṣadif to Ziyād and appointed al-Muḥājir as agent to Ṣan'ā'.[68] Ṭabarī, and following him, Ibn al-Athīr, apparently on the authority of Sayf, report that the prophet appointed Shehr b. Bādhām to Ṣan'ā', Khālid to the area between Najrān and Ṣan'ā', and al-Muḥājir to Kindah. They add that al-Muḥājir did not go on his mission during the prophet's lifetime.[69]

In addition to the three agents—Ziyād, al-Muḥājir, and 'Alī—mentioned in the report of Ibn Isḥāq, the other sources add several others who were assigned places in the area to the south of Mecca. But, among these sources also, there is disagreement concerning who was assigned where. This controversy seems to have emanated from the large number of tribes involved and the instability of the situation in the area. However, it is possible to assume that the prophet delegated many agents to Yemen, not only to collect the tax but also to propogate Islam and to try to unify the allies of Muḥammad against others.

According to Ibn Isḥāq, al-Aswad rose against al-Muḥajir, right on the latter's arrival to Yemen. The other sources confirm Ibn Isḥāq in that the rise and fall of al-Aswad took place during the prophet's lifetime.[70] There is no record to the effect that al-Aswad and his tribe adopted Islam or allied themselves with Muḥammad. On the contrary, the only report which speaks of any contact between the two denies the arrival at any agreement. The veracity of this report, however, was suspected even by the Muslim traditionists themselves.[71]

The movement of al-Aswad spread like fire. He, reportedly, captured Najrān, Ṣan'ā', and all Yemen in a few weeks.[72]

[68]Bal. *Ans.*, I, 529; Ibn Ḥabīb, 126.

[69]Ṭab., I, 1853; Athīr, II, 336.

[70]Bal. *Fut.*, I, 125, 127; Ṭab., I, 1795; 1856, 1863, 1983; Athīr, II, 340; Diyārbakrī, II, 155.

[71]Bal. *Fut.*, I, 125.

[72]Bal. *Fut.*, I, 125; Ṭab., I, 1854-55; Athīr, II, 337.

According to a report by Sayf, al-Aswad wrote to the agents of the prophet addressing them as intruding outsiders and ordering them to hand over to him whatever they had collected from Yemen. He deemed himself more entitled to the tax.[73] But the agents of the prophet fled Yemen; some went to Ḥadramawt to seek refuge with Ziyād, others went to al-Ṭāhir b. Abī Hālah, in the tribe of 'Akk, still others returned to Medina.[74]

Al-Aswad was assassinated by a group of conspirators from his entourage. The story of the assassination is narrated in Ṭabarī on the authority of Sayf, who transmitted it from 'Abd Allah son of Fayrūz al-Daylamī, a prominent member of the Abnā' and a party to the conspiracy.[75] In the way it is presented, the story is too picturesque to believe wholly. It reads like a passage from *The Thousand and One Nights;* but its essential points are confirmed by other sources. The main figures in the plot are Qays b. Makshūḥ, from the tribe of Murād, Fayrūz, and the wife of al-Aswad.

When al-Aswad captured San'ā', he is reported to have killed Shehr and married his wife.[76] Through the collaboration of this woman, the conspirators entered the house of al-Aswad and murdered him.[77] The relation between the conspirators themselves—and between them and Muḥammad—is not clear in the sources. According to Balādhurī, the prophet sent Qays to fight al-Aswad and ordered him to attract the Abnā' to his side. Together with Qays on that mission, the prophet sent Farwah b. Musayk, the chief of Murād. When the two arrived in Yemen, the news of the death of the prophet reached them. Qays, then pretended to be in agreement with al-Aswad in order that al-Aswad allow

[73]Ṭab., I, 1854.

[74]Bal. *Fut.*, I, 125; Ṭab., I, 1854-55, 1984; Athir, II, 337.

[75]Ṭab., I, 1864-68.

[76]Bal. *Fut.*, I, 126; Ṭab., I, 1855, 1864; Bayhaqi, *Sunan*, VIII, 176; Athīr, II, 337; Diyārbakrī, II, 156.

[77]Bal. *Fut.*, I, 126; Ṭab., I, 1866-67; Athīr, II, 338.

him to enter Ṣan'ā'. In Ṣan'ā', Qays organized the plot against al-Aswad; he collaborated with the Abnā' and, finally, murdered al-Aswad.[78]

Sayf b. 'Umar presents a different story as to the murder of al-Aswad. His reports are based on traditions traced back to members of the Abnā'. This probably is the reason why the Abnā', according to his version of the story, are accredited with a more glorious role in the conspiracy than Qays. Sayf claims that al-Aswad made his appearance after the Farewell Pilgrimage, when the prophet was seen to be in poor health.[79] At the same time, Qays rose against Farwah b. Musayk, the chief of Murād and the agent of the prophet in that tribe.[80] Al-Aswad appointed 'Amr b. Ma'dīkarib, a famous poet and warrior, as his agent over the tribe of Madhḥij; in Ṣan'ā' he appointed Qays as the commander of his army and Fayrūz as head of the Abnā'.[81] As soon as al-Aswad established his rule in Yemen, he started to persecute Qays and the Abnā'.[82] The prophet, then sent a letter to the Abnā' urging them to fight al-Aswad by every means. Led by Fayrūz, they undertook the task of organizing the conspiracy against al-Aswad.[83]

Both the story of Sayf and the report of Balādhurī seem to have undergone some biased editing. Traditionists doubt that Qays had ever been in contact with Muḥammad.[84] According to Ibn Isḥāq, Qays refused to join his maternal uncle 'Amr b. Ma'dīkarib on his trip to Medina.[85] In the reports about the deputation of his tribe to Medina, the name of Qays is not mentioned.[86] It is more credible that Qays

[78] Bal. *Fut.*, I, 26.
[79] Ṭab., I, 1795; Athīr, II, 337.
[80] Sa'd, I/II, 63-64; Ṭab., I, 1796; Athīr, II, 337.
[81] Ṭab., I, 1855; Athīr, II, 337.
[82] Ṭab., I, 1855, 1857 ff.; Bal. *Fut.*, I, 125-26.
[83] Ṭab., I, 1856 ff.; Athīr, II, 338 ff.
[84] Ibn Ḥajar, *Iṣābah*, III, 261; Ibn 'Abd al-Barr, 1299-1300.
[85] Isḥāq, 1004.
[86] Isḥāq, 1003; Sa'd, I/II, 63-64.

joined al-Aswad to antagonize Farwah. Farwah seems to have sought the support of Muḥammad against the tribe of Hamdān, at whose hands he had just suffered a crushing defeat.[87] The prophet appointed him as his agent over Murād, Zubayd, and Madhḥij.[88] It is most likely that as a consequence of this appointment ʻAmr suggested to his nephew Qays that he join him on a deputation to Medina to forestall any advantages that Farwah might gain over them.[89] Qays refused to join, and ʻAmr apparently failed to attain the support of the prophet against Farwah. Both Qays and ʻAmr, therefore, joined al-Aswad—as is reported by Sayf.

The Abnā', who had lost support from Persia, seem to have been willing to accept any outside backing that would enable them to retain their rule in Yemen. According to a report by al-Wāqidī, the prophet, in the year 10, sent a messenger to the Abnā' calling them to Islam; they responded and became Muslim.[90] In a report by Sayf, the same messenger is reported to have been sent by the prophet to the Abnā', urging them to fight al-Aswad.[91] In another report of Sayf's, Fayrūz and Dādhūyeh are mentioned as agents of al-Aswad over the Abnā'.[92] Balādhurī reports that al-Aswad persecuted the Abnā' when he conquered Ṣanʻā'.[93] After the death of the head of the Abnā', all sources agree that the prophet divided the rule over Yemen among many agents.[94]

In Ṣanʻā', before the dispatch of the Muslim army to Yemen under al-Muhājir, it seems that the three groups—al-Aswad and his followers, Qays and his tribesmen, and al-Abnā'—

[87]Isḥāq, 1003.

[88]Saʻd, I/II, 64; Isḥāq, 1004.

[89]Isḥāq, 1004.

[90]Ṭab., I, 1763; cf. also Watt, 121-122.

[91]Ṭab., I, 1798, 1856.

[92]Ṭab., I, 1855.

[93]Bal. *Fut.*, I, 125.

[94]Ibn Ḥabīb, I, 126; Bal. *Fut.*, I, 82-83; Bal. *Ans.*, I, 529; Ṭab., I, 1852-53; Athīr, II, 336.

were entertaining the ambitions of ruling over Yemen. None of the three had enough power by himself to assert outright his claim to authority over all the others; thus, each one was suspiciously watching the others, secretely conspiring against them, and desperately recruiting help. Qays and al-Abnā' worked together for the liquidation of al-Aswad; and, when they succeeded, they turned against each other. In the struggle between Qays and the Abnā', the former had the upper hand; he forced them out of Ṣan'ā'.[95]

Although the tradition speaks at length of the fiscal regulations which the prophet ordered his agents to follow in Yemen,[96] the issues which the tradition mentions concerning al-Aswad and Qays are not fiscal. In the sources no question of tax is raised with regard to this hostile movement against Islam in Yemen. It is evident that this movement was not a relapse from a formerly-adopted religion or a breaking of a previously-concluded alliance with Muḥammad. The survey of the source material about Yemen shows that what took place in that area at that juncture was a reaction by some local chiefs to outside interference in favor of other rival chiefs. It supports the report of Ibn Isḥāq and proves that the traditional view (that Yemen became Muslim and then apostatized) is false. The tradition, however, calls these struggles for leadership over Yemen part of the Riddah.

THE NORTH

Muḥammad's northern policy and the extent of his control over that area have been discussed in the first chapter. Ibn Isḥāq does not mention the north among the places to which the prophet sent agents to collect the tax. The vast majority among the traditional sources does not mention any movement of "apostasy" in the north. Ṭabarī and the sources based

[95] Bal. *Fut.*, I, 127; Ṭab., I, 1989-92; Athīr, II, 376.
[96] Cf. Bal. *Fut.*, I, 82-91; Abū Yūsuf, *Kharāj*, 71-75.

upon his work, however, bring up one report on the authority of Sayf to the effect that there was a Riddah in the north.[97] This report of Sayf is typical of his careless statements; it is self-contradictory and does not withstand criticism.

In the report Sayf names three agents of the prophet over tribes that had not been under Muḥammad's control. Three others are reported to have apostatized. Abū Bakr wrote to the agents commanding them to fight the "apostates"; and when Usāmah arrived, the "apostates" fled and sought refuge in Dūmat al-Jandal. This seems to be Sayf's attempt to dissimulate the failure of Usāmah's campaign. The veracity of Sayf's report is dubious; other sources do not mention any Riddah in the north, and Ibn Iṣḥāq does not mention that area as having been asked to pay the tax. It seems safe to assume that what took place in that area during the caliphate of Abū Bakr was not Riddah, but rather conquest.

* * *

This survey of the events in the different parts of Arabia shortly after the death of the prophet confirms Ibn Isḥāq's report concerning the places that were asked to pay a tax to Medina. It has been shown that, as well as to Ḥijāz which was solidly lined-up behind him, the prophet sent agents to the tribes in the north-east of Medina and into the coastal parts of Arabia. In the north-east, sections of the tribes of Ghaṭafān, Ṭayyi', and Tamīm, had agreed to pay the tax and hence their chiefs were appointed tax collectors by the prophet. In the coastal parts, the prophet recognized governors who previously were agents of the Persians and sent some of his prominent companions to these places to collect the tax. In the east, Banū Ḥanīfah were not asked to pay the tax simply because no form of agreement had been reached between them and Medina. This also was the case with the

[97] Ṭab., I, 1872; Athīr, II, 343.

major section of Asad. These conclusions, reached in this chapter, are in complete agreement with Ibn Isḥāq's report and confirm the veracity of that report. Establishing the validity of Ibn Isḥāq's report is, as has been said earlier, of prime importance for the whole problem of the Riddah. In the first place, it confirms the conclusions arrived at concerning the extent of Muḥammad's control over Arabia. Secondly, having established the validity of Ibn Isḥāq's report, it becomes possible to proceed on the basis of this report to examine which among the tribes mentioned in it did not pay the levied tax and, therefore, should be included in the Riddah, and which were not asked to pay and, therefore, should be excluded from the movement. This kind of distinction is of great significance in the question of the Riddah; especially since a Muslim army was dispatched to subdue the tribes in all these places and the tradition calls all the fighting that took place in Arabia—in the course of achieving a complete subjugation of the tribes—the Wars of al-Riddah.

In the survey preceding, it has been shown that the half-dozen movements which were crushed by the Muslim army during the caliphate of Abū Bakr were different from each other. They were not a unified front, and it can hardly be said that there was any connection between them. These movements, as has been shown, were touched off for different reasons. From the form they took and the reasons for their being, it is possible to arrange these movements into three categories. To the first category belongs the movement in Najd, where tax is the main issue; to the second, the movement of Banū Ḥanīfah, where the whole prophecy of Muḥammad and the authority of Medina over Arabia is the issue; to the third category belong the three movements in the coastal parts, where contention for leadership between local chiefs is the issue.

Of these three categories, only the first—namely, the movement in Najd, can rightly be considered Riddah: Riddah in the sense that an agreement which had been concluded with the Muslim state of Medina was broken. Here, the tribes, represented by their leaders, had entered into an agreement with the prophet and accepted the obligation of paying a tax to him. These tribes led by their chiefs violated the agreement and turned their backs on the prophet's successor. Both in concluding an agreement with Muḥammad and in breaking it with his successor, the chiefs in Najd enjoyed the support of their tribes and truly represented them. There are no signs of discord between the tribes and their chiefs. The chiefs identified their interest with the interests of their tribesmen and carried out their obligations and responsibilities towards their tribesmen faithfully. Najd is the only area from which a delegation is reported to have come to Medina to negotiate with Abū Bakr about the future of the relations between them and the state of Medina under the new leadership.

As regards the second category, represented by the tribe of Banū Ḥanīfah, there is no justification for calling their movement Riddah. In the Yamāmah, as in Najd, the tribe gave solid support to its chief and the latter faithfully represented its interests. Here no agreement had been concluded with Medina, no tax payments had been agreed on, Islam was not adopted, and the tribe was determined to keep its independence. While the tax is the issue often mentioned concerning Najd, it is the prophecy of Musaylimah and his demand to share the rule over Arabia with Medina which are the issues in point. The determination of the tribe to stand up for their interests in these two issues cannot be considered Riddah.

As for the movements of the third category (i.e., in Baḥrayn, 'Umān, and Yemen) and although each is different as a case from the other, none of these can be considered Riddah either. In these three places, the majority of the tribes did not support the chiefs who were recognized first by the Persians and later by Muḥammad. The tribes who revolted had had no contact with Muḥammad; they were revolting against their leaders who, most likely as a result of revolts, had allied themselves with Medina. In all of these places, the men who allied themselves with the prophet were on the defensive against local rivals; they never broke their alliance with Medina. In these areas, neither the allies nor their rivals broke any agreements with Medina; therefore, the term *Riddah* cannot be applied to actions of either.

In dividing the several movements in Arabia after the death of Muḥammad into these three categories, the criteria was whether those of a certain category had concluded an agreement with Muḥammad and then had broken it after his death, or not. This categorization has its parallel in the traditional sources. A few examples of how the Muslim traditionists viewed the different movements in the Riddah come next. A comparison of the different views and a collation with this study's conclusions will also be made.

* * *

The Muslim traditionists, and especially the jurists, made differentiations between movements included in the Riddah. The famous jurist, al-Shāfi'ī, says: "The apostates after the death of the prophet were of two types. Some of them are people who abandoned the religion [Islam] after having adopted it, like Ṭulayḥah, Musaylimah, al-'Ansī [al-Aswad], and their followers. The others are those who embraced Islam but withheld the tax, and they are Arabic-speaking."[98]

In a commentary on a tradition about al-Riddah, al-'Aynī, the commentator on the *Ṣaḥīḥ* of al-Bukhārī, gives a slightly different division; according to him, those who abandoned the religion after the death of the prophet fell into two categories. To the first category belong all those who apostatized from the religion, antagonized the community, and returned to their previous disbelief. They are divided into two groups. One group is made up of the followers of Musaylimah and

[98] Shāfi'ī, *al-Umm*, VIII, 255.

al-Aswad, who denied the prophethood of Muḥammad and upheld that of others. The second group is made up of those who apostatized and returned to their pre-Islamic religion. To the second category belong those who distinguished between prayer and alms-giving, embracing the first and denying the second.[99]

Diyārbakri, in *Kitāb al-Khamīs,* quotes others who differentiated between the movements which were traditionally included in the Riddah. Among them is al-Baghawī, who, in *Ma'ālim al-Tanzīl,* speaks of three groups of apostates during the illness of the prophet: in Yemen, al-Aswad, who had no previous contact with the prophet; Musaylimah, who claimed prophecy; and Ṭulayḥah, whose followers withheld the tax.[100] Another traditionist quoted by al-Diyārbakrī is al-Zuhrī, who says the following: "The apostatizing Arabs were of different groups. One group said that had [Muḥammad] been a prophet, he would not have died. Others said that the prophethood came to an end with the death of Muḥammad; we would not obey anybody else after him. Another group said we believe in God, or, we believe in God and witness that Muḥammad was his messenger, and we perform the prayer; but we will not give you [Muslims] our property.[101]

Nawbakhtī presents an interesting short resumé of the Riddah. He says:

> A group stood aloof from Abū Bakr and said: 'We will not pay the alms until we are certain of who is in command and know whom the prophet has nominated as successor. We will divide the alms among the poor and the needy of our numbers.' Another group apostatized and abandoned Islam. Banū Ḥanīfah called for the recognition of the prophethood of Musaylimah; the latter had claimed prophecy during the life of Muḥam-

[99] 'Aynī, *loc. cit.*, VIII, 244.
[100] Diyārbakrī, II, 155, 157, 160.
[101] Diyārbakrī, II, 201.

mad. Abū Bakr sent against them his cavalries under the command of Khālid b. al-Walīd al-Makhzūmī. Khālid fought them, Musaylimah was slain, others were killed, and the rest repented and acknowledged the caliphate of Abū Bakr. They therefore were called apostates, Ahl al-Riddah.[102]

These examples of views held by different Muslim authors show that they divided the "apostates" into two basic categories. The division was made along the lines of Islam's two pillars (*arkān*); one is the *shahadah* (witness) and the other is the *zakāt* (alms-giving). In the first category, they include all those who denied the prophecy of Muḥammad. Some of these authors distinguish between those who followed other prophets, such as Musaylimah, Ṭalḥah, and al-Aswad, and those who simply returned to their pre-Islamic religion. In the second category these authors include all those who withheld or refused to pay the tax.

It is obvious that the criteria according to which the Muslim authors divided the "apostates" is influenced by the authors' religious feeling. It has been shown earlier in this chapter that those whom some Muslim authors include in the first category never did adopt Islam and, hence, could not be considered to have apostatized. The inclusion of this group in the Riddah amounts to an unwarranted accusation made by Muslim authors to justify the initiation of the war against them. This war had caused bloodshed, and Muslim jurists had to find justification for bloodshed committed by those who were believed to be rightly-guided caliphs and their unerring community. By ascribing "apostasy" to these tribes, Muslim authors accounted for Abū Bakr's decision to fight them into submission.

A controversy is reported to have taken place between Abū Bakr and some prominent companions of the prophet concerning the legality of this war. The group of companoins led

[102]Nawbakhtī, *Firaq al-Shī'ah*, 4.

by 'Umar objected to Abū Bakr's decision to fight the "apostates." They based their objection on a tradition, ascribed to the prophet, to the effect that it was illegal to wage war against the tribes on the basis of the tax issue. 'Umar is reported to have said to Abū Bakr: "What right do you have to fight these people when the prophet said: 'I was ordered to fight people until they say there is no god but Allah. If they say this, they safeguard themselves and their property from me." Abū Bakr answered: "Did not he [the prophet] also say: 'except if they do not perform their duties'? Performing the prayer and paying the tax are duties incumbent upon them."[103]

Juristic arguments played a significant role in the definition of the term *Riddah* and the categorization of the groups involved in it. Shāfi'ī's writings are a prime example of how jurists twisted historical data to serve their judicial standpoints. In a section of *Kitāb al-Umm* concerning the legality of a caliph's fighting Muslim rebels, al-Shāfi'ī says: "Riddah is falling back from a previously adopted religion into disbelief and going back on the fulfillment of previously accepted duties." After this definition of *Riddah*, al-Shāfi'ī proceeds to mention the argument between Abū Bakr and 'Umar concerning the legality of the war. He claims that both Abū Bakr and 'Umar knew that there were Muslims among those whom they were fighting. Otherwise, 'Umar would not have had any doubts as to the legality of waging that war and Abū Bakr would have said "they abandoned 'there is no god but Allah' and became idolators." The allegation that 'Umar agreed eventually with Abū Bakr was proof for Shāfi'ī that rebels should be fought even if they be Muslims.[104]

Shāfi'ī's definition of the Riddah, his categorization of the groups involved, and his inclusion of them all in the Riddah are obvious distortions of historical data. He included all the

[103]With some variations, this dialogue is found in Shāf'ī, *al-Umm*, VIII, 255; Jāhiz, *al-'Uthmānīyah*, 81; Baghdādī, *al-Farq bayn al-firaq*, 16; Bayhaqī, *Sunan*, VIII, 176; Diyārbakrī, 201; Ibn Kathīr, VI, 311.

[104]Shāfi'ī, al-Umm, VIII, 255-256.

different groups in the Riddah in order to formulate a definition that might justify Abū Bakr's waging war against the "apostates." By establishing the legality of Abū Bakr's action, al-Shāfi'ī aimed at supporting his juristic point of view concerning Muslim rebels in general.

'Aynī who presents a slightly different division as that of Shāfi'ī by adding the following concerning the second category: "Those [the withholders of the tax] are, in reality, rebels. They were not called by this name at that time in particular because they were mixed with the apostates. The term *apostasy* was applied to all those groups because it was the more important and serious." In distinction from al-Shāfi'ī, al-'Aynī is hesitant to include the withholders of the tax in the Riddah. From the context, there is no indication that al-'Aynī is trying to support a given point of view, but he points out the carelessness that was practiced in the application of the term *Riddah.*

In the context of factional political argument concerning the preference of Abū Bakr over 'Alī for the caliphate, Ibn Abī al-Ḥadīd, the commentator on *Nahj al-balāghah*, gives the following comment on the Riddah: "[the withholders of the tax] were not apostates, they were called so by the companions of the prophet by way of metaphor. The companions called them that name because they deemed what the withholders of the tax said and how they interpreted the *Koran* a great sin.[105]

While al-Shāfi'ī had no hesitation about including both categories in the Riddah, al-'Aynī hesitated to include those of the second (tax withholders) and the Muslim historians hesitated to include those of the first category. All the historical sources agree that what took place in Najd after the death of the prophet was Riddah.[106] As regards the tribes in Najd, the sources are clear about the issue and talk about a concrete

[105]Ibn Asi al-Ḥadid, XIII, 187.

[106]Bal. *Fut.*, I, 113-114; Ṭab., I, 1871; Athir, II, 342 ff.; Diyārbakrī, II, 201-202.

problem, i.e., the tax. With regard to other places the issue is vague, and the historians call the tribes there "apostates" but not without reluctance. Ibn al-Athīr treats the rise of al-Aswad separately from the rest of the "apostates" and does not call his movement Riddah.[107] Balādhurī includes the movement of al-Aswad in the Riddah, but he does not say that al-Aswad apostatized. The title of the chapter in which Balādhurī treats the movement of al-Aswad reads as follows: "The affair of al-Aswad al-'Ansī and those who apostatized with him in Yemen." However, in the discussion, Balāduri does not mention anyone as having adopted Islam and then having apostatized.[108]

As regards Musaylimah, Balādhurī treats his movement separately from his consideration of the Riddah. He mentions some apostatizing individuals in Musaylimah's entourage, but does not say that either Banū Ḥanīfah as a whole or Musaylimah himself apostatized. Balādhurī also makes a distinction between the war with the tribes in Najd and that with Banū Ḥanīfah. He says: "When the prophet died and Abū Bakr was elected caliph and subjugated the apostates in Najd and its surroundings in a few months, he [Abū Bakr] sent Khālid b. al-Walīd and ordered him to fight Musaylimah the Liar."[109] Ibn al-Athīr, however, includes Banū Ḥanīfah and Musaylimah among the apostatizing tribes whom Abū Bakr sent armies to subjugate.[110] The reports of Sayf b. 'Umar, which were preserved in Ṭabarī, indict all those who were involved in the fighting in Arabia after the death of the prophet with apostasy.[111] These reports have been discussed and criticized earlier in this chapter.

* * *

[107]Athīr, II, 336-342.
[108]Bal. *Fut.*, I, 125-127.
[109]Bal. *Fut.*, I, 105-112.
[110]Athīr, II, 360.
[111]Ṭab., I, 1738-39, 1795-96, 1851-69, 1870 ff., events of the year 11 A.H.

This confusion in the historical sources concerning the application of the term *Riddah* to the movements in Arabia after the prophet's death confirms 'Aynī, who pointed out the carelessness of the application of the term.[112] The historians seem to have disregarded the causes of these movements and were concerned mainly with accounting for the war against them. This war was carried out in a short time. It aimed at complete subjugation of the tribes, regardless of their past relations with Medina. The war was one and the same against all the movements, and the name Riddah gained prevalence for it. The name of the war decided that given to the warriors and their movements. 'Aynī's comment seems to be correct. The term *Riddah* was used carelessly by Muslim historians; they, however, do not seem to have meant it in the same elaborate and complicated sense that jurists later attributed to the term. But once the mistake was made, traditionists, jurists, those who wrote about heresy, and the mouthpieces of political factions twisted it to serve their own purposes. It seems most likely to have originated as a term to indicate the behavior of the tribes to the north-east of Medina who failed to fulfill their duties towards the Muslim state. The storytellers (of Sayf b. 'Umar's type) and, following them, the early historians extended the term carelessly to all the movements in Arabia—mainly because the war against them all was one and the same and was carried out in a very short time. The jurists switched the designation of the term by emphatically applying it to those who never did, in fact, adopt Islam.

To sum up then, it seems that the Riddah was originally limited to the tribes to the northeast of Medina, i.e., Ghaṭafān, Tayyi', and Tamīm. Those tribes were called *Ahl al-Riddah*, "backsliders," because they withheld the tax which they had promised to pay to Muḥammad. The term *Riddah* was then extended to all the movements which took place in Arabia following the death of the prophet. The term was later twisted

[112] 'Aynī, *loc. cit.*, VIII, 243.

to serve juristic arguments and opinions and was then adopted in its juristic sense by later historians.

4. THE RIDDAH AND THE ARAB CONQUEST

Muslim traditionists considered all antagonists of Medina "apostates" and called the war waged against them the War of Apostasy, *Hurūb al-Riddah.* In the light of the conclusions reached in the previous chapter, however, only the operations of those who withheld the tax can properly be designated as Riddah. Muslim campaigns against all others must be considered conquest. Whether or not there was any relation between the Riddah and the conquest is the next question that arises.

To confirm the conclusion that the war in Arabia, outside of north-eastern Najd, was a war of conquest and to deal with considerations that arise from this conclusion, a survey of that war and a collation of the traditional reports concerning it are essential. In the following pages, a comprehensive presentation of the war of al-Riddah and an attempt to draw some conclusions concerning its relation to the Arab conquest movement will be made.

* * *

The Campaign of Usāmah

It has been said that this campaign was prepared by the prophet himself after his return from the Farewell Pilgrimage;

but that, before the army departed to its destination on the Syrian border, the prophet died.[1] The squabble in Medina concerning the successor to the prophet had repercussions on Usāmah's expedition. Nevertheless, the traditional sources emphasize the concern and the seriousness of Abū Bakr's purpose in carrying out the prophet's plan and in dispatching Usāmah's army.[2] In the sources, over-emphasis of Abū Bakr's determination to dispatch this army as the prophet had ordered is probably greatly influenced by religious feelings. The traditionists wanted to show how much the first caliph esteemed and venerated the prophet's word and will. However, it is quite obvious from the same sources' descriptions of the expedition that the campaign was not carried out quite as it was originally planned.

Balādhurī counts the expedition of Usāmah among the *sarāyā*[3] the prophet himself ordered. His account is brief and little information can be derived from it.[4] Ya'qūbī is even sketchier, and the only piece of information he gives is that the duration of the expedition was "sixty or forty" days.[5] Ibn al-Athīr's report, which is based on that of al-Ṭabarī,[6] is more informative concerning the preparation and destination of the expedition. The reports of Ibn al-Athīr supply the following information: The prophet ordered the Muslims to prepare for an attack on Syria in al-Muḥarram, the first

[1]Cf. Chapter I.

[2]'Asākir, I, 433 ff.; Bal. *Ans.*, I, 384; Ṭab., I, 1848 ff.; Athīr, II, 334; Ya'qūbī, II, 127.

[3]*Sarāyā* (sing. *sarīyah*) is a raiding party. The term is used in the tradition to designate the small raiding companies in which the prophet did not take part. The campaigns of the prophet are known by the term *maghāzī* (sing. *ghazāh* or *ghazwah*). *Sarīyah* is derived from the root *Sarā*, 'to travel by night."

[4]Bal. *Ans.*, I, 384.

[5]Ya'qūbī, II, 127.

[6]Ṭabarī's report is based partly on Ibn Isḥāq but mostly on Sayf b. 'Umar; cf. Ibn al-Athīr, II, 317, with Ṭab., I, 1794, and Isḥāq, 1025, 1056.

month, of the year 11. The "hypocrites" complained about the nomination of Usāmah as commander; the prophet scolded them. In one place, Ibn al-Athīr mentions that the early Muhājirūn, Abū Bakr, 'Umar, and others were all in the army of Usāmah; while the people were preparing for the campaign, the prophet's illness began.[7] In another place, Ibn al-Athīr mentions only 'Umar and omits Abū Bakr as having been in the army of Usāmah. He adds: when Abū Bakr ordered the army to march, it was the Anṣār who complained about Usāmah; 'Umar brought the complaint to Abū Bakr, who refused to change the orders of the prophet. Abū Bakr asked Usāmah to release 'Umar from the army to stay in Medina and help him execute his duties. Usāmah attacked some tribes on the Syrian borders who had apostatized, defeated them, won much booty, and then returned to Medina.[8]

Those reports which are based on al-Wāqidī's works concerning the campaign of Usāmah are different. According to Wāqidī, the prophet ordered the Muslims to prepare for an attack on the Byzantines at the end of Ṣafar (the second month) of the year 11. Usāmah was nominated commander and was ordered to attack those who had killed his father. The prominent Muhājirūn and the Anṣār—Abū Bakr, 'Umar, Abū 'Ubaydah, Sa'd b. Abī Waqqāṣ, Sa'īd b. Zayd, Qatādah b. al-Nu'mān, Salamah b. Aslam—were in the army. Wāqidī mentions the complaints about the appointment of Usāmah as commander but he does not specify who complained. He also does not mention the complaint of the Anṣār when Abū Bakr dispatched the army. In an eloquent passage, al-Wāqidī describes Usāmah's attack on Ubnā in southern Jordan. He killed, avenged his father's blood, burned, captured, plundered, and returned safely.[9]

An interesting report on the authority of Sayf is given by

[7]Athīr, II, 317.
[8]Athīr, II, 334 ff.
[9]Sa'd, II/I, 136; 'Asākir, I, 435-39.

Ibn 'Asākir and Ṭabarī. According to this report, tribes on the Syrian border apostatized. Abū Bakr urged those who remained loyal to Islam to fight them. Then when Usāmah arrived, the apostates fled; Usāmah raisded al-Ḥamqatayn and Abil and returned safely and with much booty.[10]

A comparison of the different reports and a scrutiny of the individual accounts betray the traditionists' efforts to cover-up the failure of Usāmah's expedition to accomplish its goal. To consider it a *sarīyah* is to account for the result and to ignore the motivation behind the conception of this campaign and the goal it was hoped it would achieve. Reports treating Usāmah's campaign as a *sarīyah* contradict other reports which speak of it as a big campaign against the Byzantines.

The flowery rhetoric concerning the success of the expedition, telling in broad terms of victory and much booty, is probably meant to prove that Usāmah was worthy of the task he was entrusted with by the prophet. The over-emphasized insistance of Abū Bakr to dispatch the army under the command of Usāmah, in spite of the opposition he encountered, seems to be an easy way of demonstrating Abū Bakr's deep veneration of Muḥammad. But what of 'Umar and the Anṣār: did they not hold the same respect for the prophet? The army is reported to have included the Muhājirūn and the Anṣār. When it was dispatched, Abū Bakr asked Usāmah to release only 'Umar; all the rest supposedly remained with the army. But this contradicts other reports on events which took place in Medina during the absence of Usāmah and his army—since the names of those who were supposed to be with Usāmah are mentioned as having taken part in those events. The early companions were commanders of the guards of Medina during the absence of Usāmah and were with Abū Bakr when he went to Dhū al-Qaṣṣah to fight the apostates before the return of Usāmah to Medina.[11]

[10]Ṭab., I, 1872-73; 'Asākir, I, 432-33; al-Ḥamqatayn and Abil are places in Southern Jordan.

[11]See Ṭab., I, 1874; Diyārbakrī, II, 201-202, 204.

According to Wāqidī, the army of Usāmah was made up of 3,000 men; others put the figure at 700.[12] Caetani tends to accept the lesser number as more reasonable.[13] He is most likely right, considering the outcome of the expedition. But even were the greater number to be accepted, it is still smaller by far than the numbers participating in the campaign to Tabūk; and so it is very unlikely that it was sent against the Byzantines. This army evidently did not include all of the Anṣār, the Muhājirūn and the tribes in the area surrounding Mecca and Medina. Moreover, it is highly improbable that the opposition party among the Anṣār participated in the campaign.

All signs indicate that the expedition of Usāmah started as an out-growth of Tabūk, a major campaign of Muḥammad's against the Arab tribes in southern Syria. The death of the prophet and the squabbles among his followers caused the campaign to falter and end as an insignificant raid. The participants in this raid were most probably the group of *Ahl al-Ṣuffah* for whom Abū Bakr found himself obliged to provide, as had the prophet before him. Traditionists, trying hard to whitewash the failure of the campaign and the controversy in Medina, wanted to show the early Muslim community in the best possible light. In spite of Usāmah's fiasco, the invasion of Syria remained Abū Bakr's major objective through the ensuing events in Arabia, as will be seen.

Sayf's story that Usāmah's campaign was directed against apostates in the north should be discounted, since this campaign was prepared before the death of the prophet and before the Riddah had started. No other source ascribes to Usāmah's campaign such motives as Sayf gives. The importance of Sayf's report is that it shows to what extent the excuse of "apostasy" has been used to dissimulate the motives for agressive Muslim military activity.

[12]'Asākir, I, 438, 440.
[13]Caetani, *Annali*, II/I, 587-88.

Dhū al-Qaṣṣah

The battle of Dhū al-Qaṣṣah took place shortly after Abū Bakr was elected caliph.[14] Caetani thinks it was in Jumādā II (sixth month) of the year 11.[15] According to a report on the authority of Abū Ma'shar, Abū Bakr did not initiate any military activity during the absence of Usāmah and his army from Medina. The campaign of Usāmah lasted forty days or, according to other versions, seventy. Meanwhile, delegations representing the "apostatizing" tribes came to Medina to negotiate new agreements with Abū Bakr. The delegates requested to be exempted from the payment of the tax and pledged to continue to perform the prayer. Abū Bakr rejected their request and waited for the return of Usāmah before launching an attack on those tribes. When Usāmah arrived in Medina, Abū Bakr led the Muslim army to Dhū al-Qaṣṣah, where he encountered Khārijah b. Ḥiṣn al-Fazārī. Ṭabarī, who preserved this report of Abū Ma'shar, does not elaborate further and satisfied himself by saying: "Abū Bakr hid in a bush, then God defeated the infidels."[16]

Other reports preserved in Ṭabarī, especially those transmitted on the authority of Sayf b. 'Umar, add more details to the story of Dhū al-Qaṣah. According to Sayf, the camp of the "apostates" in Dhū al-Qaṣṣah was only one of several camps where the allied forces of Ghaṭafān, Asad, and Ṭayyi' were assembled in preparation for a confrontation with the Muslims.[17] The arrival in Medina of a delegation to negotiate with Abū Bakr is confirmed by Sayf. He adds, however, that the delegates took lodgings with the notables of the town. Al-Abbās, fore-father of the dynasty under whom Sayf wrote, was the only one who did not give lodgings to any members of the delegation. The notables supported the delegates in their

[14]Cf. also Caetani, *Annali*, II/I, 592-99; Wellhausen, *Skizzen*, VI, 8.
[15]Caetani, *Annali*, II/I, 556.
[16]Ṭab., I, 1870; see also Caetani, *Annali*, II/I, 592.
[17]Ṭab., I, 1874; Athīr, II, 344.

request to be exempted from paying the tax: but Abū Bakr flatly rejected that request.[18]

In the same report, Sayf tells that, when it was apparent that the delegation's mission had failed, the delegates returned to their tribes and informed them of the sparcity of population in Medina. This induced some tribes to stage a surprise attack on Medina. The invaders left their reinforcement behind in Dhū Ḥusā and proceeded towards the town. The Medinans, under the command of Abū Bakr, repelled the invaders and pursued them. At Dhū Ḥusā, the Muslims were ambushed by the reinforcement, which startled the camels of the Muslims with inflated skin bags. The Muslims dispersed at first but reassembled soon to stage a counter-attack and win a victory —which according to Sayf was won before Usāmah's return from Syria—strengthened the hand of Muslims everywhere. Upon the arrival of Usāmah in Medina, Abū Bakr attacked another camp of the allies in a place called al-Abraq.[19] Sayf, in this report, contradicts Abū Ma'shar who claims that no fighting took place between the Muslims and the "apostates" during the absence of Usāmah.

Not only does Abū Ma'shar's report contradict Sayf's; those based on the works of al-Wāqidī do so, too. A résumé of al-Wāqidī's version of the story goes as follows:[20] The delegation which came to Medina was led by 'Uyaynah b. Ḥiṣn al-Fazārī and al-Aqra' b. Ḥābis al-Tamīmī. The delegates told Abū Bakr that the tribes in their areas had apostatized and were not willing to pay the tax; but, were Abū Bakr to grant an allowance to 'Uyaynah and al-Aqra', the delegates would save the Muslims the trouble of dealing with those tribes. Both Muhājirūn and Anṣār urged Abū Bakr to accept the offer and the conditions of the delegation; but he refused

[18] Ṭab., I, 1874; Athīr, II, 344.
[19] Ṭab., I, 1878; Athīr, II, 345.
[20] This report is given without *isnād* in Diyārbakrī, II, 202-4. The same report is given in Caetani's *Annali*, II/I, 592-93, on the authority of al-Wāqidī from the Ms. of Ibn Ḥubaysh.

and insisted on fighting the apostates.

As regards the encounter with Khārijah b. Ḥiṣn, al-Wāqidī presents this story: When Abū Bakr's resolution to fight the apostates was adopted, he led a small army of the Muhājirūn and the Anṣār to Dhū al-Qaṣṣah. He also sent messengers to some loyal tribes calling them to come to his aid. At Dhū al-Qaṣṣah, Abū Bakr ordered the Muslims to camp and wait for the reinforcement; meanwhile, Khārijah, who was on his way to Medina to dissuade people from joining Abū Bakr, staged a surprise attack on the Muslim camp. The Muslims, caught unaware, dispersed in confusion; and Abū Bakr hid in a bush. The Muslims reassembled, however, and with some reinforcements staged a counterattack and defeated the enemy, who fled leaving one person dead on the battlefield. Abū Bakr remained a few days in Dhū al-Qaṣṣah waiting for the Muslim tribes to arrive. Detachments from Aslam, Ghifār, Muzaynah, Ashja', Juhaynah, and Ka'b came to Dhū al-Qaṣṣah answering to Abū Bakr's call.[21] Diyārbakrī, quoting other sources, gives many reports to the effect that some prominent early Muhājirūn disagreed with Abū Bakr's decision to fight the withholders of the tax.[22]

Balādhurī's report on Dhū al-Qaṣṣah agrees generally with that of al-Wāqidī. In his version of the story, Balādhurī mentions the arrival in Medina of a delegation to negotiate with Abū Bakr, the companions' reluctance to fight the Arab tribes, and Abū Bakr's insistance on procuring the tax even if by force. As regards the encounter with Khārijah, al-Balādhurī gives the following: Abū Bakr went to Dhū al-Qaṣṣah in order to organize his armies there and to dispatch them against the apostates. Khārijah and Manzūr b. Zabbān and a group of Ghaṭafānīs attacked the Muslims. The two parties fought a fierce battle; the infidels were defeated; one

[21]Diyārbakrī, II, 204; Caetani, Annali, II/I, 593.

[22]Diyārbakrī, II, 201. See also Bal. *Fut.*, I, 113; al-Muvarrad, *Kāmil*, I, 390-91; Bayhaqī, *Sunan*, VIII, 176.

person was killed; and the rest ran away.[23]

From these reports, it is evident that the "battle of Dhū al-Qaṣṣah" was only a small skirmish between the vanguard of the Muslim army and a splinter of the tribe of Ghaṭafān. But, in spite of the insignificance of Dhū al-Qaṣṣah as a battle, the reports concerning it point out two episodes of prime importance as far as the Riddah is concerned. The first episode is the arrival in Medina of a delegation from the tribes to the north-east of Medina. And the second is the disagreement within the Muslim community concerning the war against the withholders of the tax.

The arrival in Medina of a delegation to negotiate a new agreement with Abū Bakr confirms the conclusions drawn in the previous chapter regarding the extent and character of the Riddah. That these tribes were willing to negotiate indicates that they were not anxious to sever absolutely their relations with Medina. The demands of the delegation also confirm the conclusion that the issue behind the Riddah was the tax.

The second episode, i.e., the disagreement of the companions with Abū Bakr's policy, has its implications as regards the factional antagonisms within the Muslim community in Medina. Abū Bakr could not have stood alone in the face of the opposition party. As to who were the supporters of Abū Bakr's policy, the sources are not explicit, but there are many indications that they were the newly-converted Meccans. In this survey of the war, the opposition to Abū Bakr will be pointed out in the context of the episode as it arises; but, it will be treated separately in the following chapter.

* * *

The traditional reports concerning what happened after Dhū al-Qaṣṣah are confused and in many cases contradictory;

[23]Bal. *Fut.*, I, 113-114.

different authors present various stories, and quite often the same author gives different versions of the same story. The confusion seems to have been caused by the multitude of military activities in Arabia occurring within a very short period of time and by the authors' reconciliation of a large number of orally transmitted accounts of a single event. The most prevalent version of the story, however, is that of Sayf b. 'Umar. It was adopted by Ṭabarī and, following him, by later historians.

From Sayf's story it is learned that Abū Bakr, after the engagement with Khārijah, fought and defeated two more camps of the allied tribes of Najd: 'Abs and Dhubyān, subtribes of Ghaṭafān.[24] Then, when Usāmah returned and his army had rested, Abū Bakr went to Dhū al-Qaṣṣah and from there dispatched eleven armies, supposedly at the same time, to all parts of Arabia to subjugate the "apostatizing" tribes.[25] There follows a list of the commanders of these armies and their destinations: (1) Khālid b. al-Walīd was entrusted with the command of the army which was sent to fight Ṭalḥah and his allies, and to fight Malik b. Nuwayrah, thereafter; (2) 'Ikrimah b. Abī Jahl was sent against Banū Ḥanīfah; (3) al-Muhājir b. Abī Umayyah was sent against the remnants of the army of al-Aswad and was ordered to help al-Abnā' against Qays b. Makshūḥ; (4) Khālid b. Sa'īd was dispatched to al-Ḥamqatayn on the Syrian border; (5) 'Amr b. al-'Aṣ was dispatched to southern Palestine, where the tribe of Quḍā'ah was settled; (6) Ḥudhayfah b. Miḥṣan was assigned to Dabbā in 'Umān; (7) 'Arfajah b. Harthamah was assigned to Mahrah; (8) Shuraḥbīl b. Ḥasanah was sent to reinforce 'Ikrimah in Yamāmah and was ordered to join 'Amr in Quḍā'ah thereafter; (9) Ṭurayfah b. Ḥājizah was assigned to the tribe of Sulaym and to those who lived among them from Hawāzin; (10) Suwayd b. al-Muqarrin was sent to Tihāmah, the coastal

[24] Ṭlb., I, 1876, 1879; Athīr, II, 345.
[25] Ṭab., I, 1880-81; Athīr, II, 346.

part on the Red Sea of Yemen; (11) al-'Alā' b. al-Ḥaḍramī was dispatched to Baḥrayn.

Throughout the following survey of the war of al-Riddah, this report of Sayf's and his version of the various events will be collated with the reports of other authorities in an attempt to present a comprehensive story of the war, based on all the available information. Sayf is almost exclusively Ṭabarī's authority on the Riddah. Ṭabarī's account is the most complete and detailed version among the extant sources. But, as he preserved it, Ṭabarī's version still suffers from Sayf's own biases and prejudices, and it leaves many gaps, especially with regard to the activities of commanders other than Khālid b. al-Walīd. Sayf was a Tamīmī, and his tribe fought in the ranks of the Muslim army under Khālid's command. This might explain why Khālid's exploits are described at length and in detail in Sayf's reports at the expense of the other commanders' activities. The works of other authorities, on the other hand, have not reached us in a complete and coherent form; only fragments of these other works, scattered in various sources, were preserved. Therefore, the method which will be employed in the survey is one of criticism of Sayf's reports in the light of the information supplied by others, where possible. Where Sayf fails to answer the questions that arise, an attempt will be made to piece the various fragments of information together and to reconcile them against the background of the conclusions made in the previous chapters.

al-Buzākhah

Like Dhū al-Qaṣṣah, the battle of al-Buzākhah was named after the area where it was fought. It took place shortly after Dhū al-Qaṣṣah; Caetani believes: at the end of Rajab (seventh month) or the beginning of Sha'bān (eighth month) of the year 11.[26] All traditional sources agree that Khālid b. al-Walīd was the commander of the Muslim army and that

[26]Caetani, *Annali*, II/I, 557.

Ṭalḥah was in command of the allied forces of the tribes of Najd—Asad, Ṭayyi', and Ghaṭafān—who fought the battle against the Muslim army.[27] There is disagreement, however, among the traditionists concerning who were the allies. Wāqidī and Ibn Isḥāq and those who followed them exclude Ṭayyi' and mention only Ghaṭafān as allied to Ṭalḥah, who was from the tribe of Asad.[28] Sayf on the other hand claims that both Ghaṭafān and Ṭayyi' allied themselves with Ṭalḥah.[29] But both Sayf and al-Wāqidī agree that before the arrival of Khālid to al-Buzākhah, 'Adīy b. Ḥātim, a chief from Ṭayyi', mediated between him and the different subtribes of Ṭayyi' and succeeded in detaching them from the allied camp and drawing them to Khālid's side against their former allies.[30] On the battlefield, Khālid, with the Muslim army from Medina and the new allies from Ṭayyi', won a decisive victory over the two allies, Ṭalḥah and 'Uyaynah b. Ḥiṣn, from Asad and Ghaṭafān respectively. Ṭalḥah is reported to have fled to Syria, while 'Uyaynah was captured and sent to Medina.[31]

The battle of Buzākhah is a prime example of the Muslim strategy during the wars in Arabia. This war was carried out mainly by local forces, recruited from the tribes in the surroundings of that particular battlefield. The Muslim army that was dispatched from Medina, if any, was usually relatively small and always relied on forces recruited at its destination. Sayf reports that before the departure of Khālid to al-Buzākhah, Abū Bakr delegated 'Adīy b. Ḥātim to his tribe (Ṭayyi') in an attempt to dissuade his tribesmen from joining

[27]Bal. *Fut.*, I, 114-115; Ṭab., I, 1886; Bayhaqī, *Sunan*, VIII, 187; Athīr, II, 347; Diyārbakrī, II, 207.

[28]Bal. *Fut.*, I, 115, 116; Ṭab., I, 1889; 'Aynī, *loc. cit.*, VIII, 244-45; Diyārbakrī, II, 202, 205; Caetani, *Annali*, II/I, 611.

[29]Ṭab., I, 1892-93; Athīr, II, 344.

[30]Ṭab., I, 1887; Athīr, II, 346-47; Diyārbakrī, II, 205; Caetani, *Annali*, II/I, 611.

[31]Bal. *Fut.*, I, 115; Ṭab., I, 1891, 1896; Diyārbakrī, II, 207.

Ṭalḥah; 'Adīy succeeded in his mission. Sayf adds: When Khālid marched, he pretended to be heading towards Khaybar; this stratagem confused the enemy, forced Ṭayyi' to remain in their territory to defend it, and thus prevented them from joining Ṭalḥah in al-Buzākhah. 'Adīy, then, mediated between Khālid and Ṭayyi' and succeeded in detaching both sub-tribes of Ṭayyi'—Ghawth and Jadīlah—from the allied forces.[32] According to a report by Hishām b. al-Kalbī, 'Adīy urged Khālid to make his way through the territory of Ṭayyi' and pledged to recruit for the Muslim army as many warriors as Khālid had.[33] Whether voluntarily or under the threat of attack, Ṭayyi' was easily detached from the camp of the allies, most likely because of their old animosity to both Ghaṭafān and Asad.[34]

After the victory in al-Buzākhah, Khālid dispatched detachments of his army in several directions; remnants of the camp of al-Buzākhah were defeated; and the tribe of 'Amir b. Ṣa'ṣa'ah, a branch of Hawāzin, were constrained to seek a peaceful surrender to the Muslims.[35] Diyārbakrī gives the following description of the situation in central Najd after al-Buzākhah:

> The Arabs began to flock to Khālid out of desire to adopt Islam or from fear of the sword. Some were captured and claimed either that they had come voluntarily to submit to Islam or that they had never apostatized but rather had been stingy with their property and now would willingly pay their dues. Others, who were not captured, either came to Khālid yielding to Islam or headed to Medina to submit to Abū Bakr, avoiding Khālid.[36]

[32]Ṭab., I, 1886-87. Athīr, II, 346-47.

[33]Ṭab., I, 1888.

[34]Ṭab., I, 1893.

[35]Bal. *Fut.*, I, 116-117; Ṭab., I, 1899-1906; Athīr, II, 349-352; cf. also, Caetani, *Annali*, II/I, 619-625.

[36]Diyārbakrī, II, 208; cf. also, Ibn al-Athīr, II, 349-350; Ṭab., I, 1899-1906.

In conclusion, it is possible to assume that the battle of al-Buzākhah brought all central Najd under the direct control of Medina for the first time.

From Sayf's report on the dispatch of eleven armies against the apostates and his reports on al-Buzākhah, it is understood that only a portion of the Muslim army was with Khālid; the rest set out in different directions, and the assumption is that fighting was going on in different fronts simultaneously. This is not, however, what other sources claim. Balādhurī, for instance, does not speak of eleven armies having been dispatched by Abū Bakr, but he reports that Abū Bakr went to Dhū al-Qaṣṣah to organize and dispatch armies against the apostates. Without mentioning where the army was recruited, al-Balādhurī makes the following statement: "Abū Bakr, while in Dhū al-Qaṣṣah, nominated Khālid b. al-Walīd commander of the army [supposedly all of it] and appointed Thābit b. Qays commander of the Anṣār; Thābit, however, was under Khālid. Abū Bakr ordered Khālid to hold out firmly against Ṭalḥah."[37] Other sources also indicate that Khālid led the whole Muslim army to al-Buzākhah and do not speak of eleven armies.[38] This controversy will be examined below.

Al-Buṭāḥ

The battle of al-Buṭāḥ is also named for the place where the battle was fought. Caetani puts it near the end of year 11. But al-Buṭāḥ was not a battle in the real sense; it was more of a raid by the cavalry of Khālid on the camp of Yarbūʿ, a sub-tribe of Tamīm. In this raid, Mālik b. Nuwayrah, chief of Yarbūʿ, was captured and put to death.[40] No more fighting

[37]Bal. *Fut.*, I, 114. This report of Balādhurī seems to have originated in the works of Hishām b. al-Kalbī; see Ṭab., 6, 1887.

[38]Shāfiʿī, *al-Umm*, VIII, 256; Tab., I, 1887; Diyārbakri, II, 205; Caetani, *Annali*, II/I, 600.

[39]Caetani, *Annali*, II/I, 557.

[40]Bal. *Fut.*, I, 117; Ṭab., I, 1925-26; *Aghānī*, XV, 239-245; Wathīmah, 12; Baghdādī, *Khizānah*, I, 236; Ibn al-Athīr, II, 358-59; Diyārbakrī, II, 209.

is reported to have taken place between the Muslim army and any other tribe from Tamīm.

The story of Mālik's death has always captured the attention of the traditionists; they narrate it at length, neglecting other events among Tamīm during the Riddah. In the extant sources, the story is given in several variant versions. All versions are in agreement that Khālid put Mālik to death, but they disagree as to the reason. The variety of reasons—as supplied in the tradition in support of or in apposition to Khālid's conduct in this event—range from his coveting Mālik's wife,[41] who reportedly was very beautiful, to his religiously tinctured argument with Mālik about the prophethood of Muḥammad.[42] The story of Mālik's death seems to have gained its prominence in the annals of the Riddah because of the famous elegies of Mutammim, the poet-bother of Mālik, who reportedly kept weeping and reciting poetry on the death of his brother until he lost his eye-sight.[43] Also, the juristic controversy as to whether Khālid's marriage to Mālik's wife was lawful or not contributed much to the currency of the story.[44]

As for the Riddah among the rest of Tamīm, the tradition is cryptic and supplies only fragmentary information. This seems to be due to the fact that Sayf b. 'Umar, Ṭabarī's principal authority, belonged to Tamīm and was anxious to present his tribe in the best possible light. Sayf claims that the jealous leaders of Tamīm were split among themselves with regard to the prophetess Sajāḥ[45] and with regard to the tribe's relation to Medina. As a result of the death of Muḥammad and the appearance of Sajāḥ amongst them, parts of Tamīm joined with Sajāḥ while others decided to fulfill their obligations to Medina; a fraternal war was, thus, touched off within the

[41]Wathīmah, 12; *Aghānī*, XV, 239.
[42]Ṭab., I, 1928; Diyārbakrī, II, 209.
[43]Bal. *Fut.*, I, I, 118; Athīr, II, 359.
[44]Cf. also Caetani, *Annali*, II/I, 656-58.
[45]*E. I.*, article "Sadjaḥ" by V. Vacca.

tribe.[46] Other sources, however, claim that all of Tamīm apostatized.[47] But, except for the raid on al-Buṭāḥ, there is no mention in the sources of any fighting between the Muslims and Tamīm. It seems that the tribes of Tamīm, after a period of reluctance and under threat of attack by Khālid, yielded to the Muslim army after its victory in al-Buzākhah.[48]

The traditional accounts of al-Buṭāḥ point out two significant episodes which shed light on the political factionalism in the Muslim camp at that time and on the atttitudes of the different groups towards the war of al-Riddah. The first episode is the reluctance of the Anṣār to carry on in the war and the second is the opposition to Khālid's conduct of the war. The Anṣār are reported to have objected to Khālid's resolution to attack Tamīm. This objection was, according to some authors, based on the pretext that Abū Bakr had not authorized such an attack. Khālid, however, claimed to have been authorized by the caliph and declared that he would not oblige anybody to follow him. The Anṣār, eventually, gave in and joined Khālid.

Diyārbakrī, probably on the authority of al-Wāqidī, claims that the Anṣār complained of fatigue and lack of adequate forces to continue in the war.[50] Sayf reports that Khālid's reaction to the objection of the Anṣār was his resolution to march on the territory of Tamīm regardless of whether or not the Anṣār went along with him. Khālid replied to his opponents that he was the commander and, even if he were not authorized by the caliph when a good opportunity presented itself, he would not let his hand slip just to get the caliph's approval.[51] Whatever the arguments on the two sides might have been, it is the episode itself and its implications that

[46]Ṭab., I, 1909, 1911.
[47]Ṭab., I, 1919; Diyārbakrī, II, 202; 'Aynī, *loc. cit*., VIII, 244.
[48]Ṭab., I, 1909-1910.
[49]Ṭab., I, 1922; Athīr, II, 357; Diyārbakrī, II, 209.
[50]Diyārbakrī, II, 209.
[51]Ṭab., I, 1923; Athīr, II, 357.

concerns the discussion at this point. If the Anṣār were reluctant to join Khālid and he was resolute to march on Tamīm, the question is: on what forces was he relying?

It is most unlikely that Khālid would have marched on the land of Tamīm without, at least, the tacit approval of Abū Bakr. Sayf claims that Abū Bakr dispatched Khālid from Dhū al-Qaṣṣah with clear-cut orders to march on Tamīm after having subjugated Ṭalḥah and his allies in al-Buzākhah.[52] Balādhurī is explicit only with regard to Abū Bakr's authorization of Khālid to fight Ṭalḥah; as for Khālid's other military activity, al-Balādhurī does not raise the question of authorization. Balādhurī reports on the fighting with Tamīm without further mention of the question.[53] Diyārbakrī reports that Khālid, after the victory in al-Buzākhah, pretended that Abū Bakr had sanctioned the attack on Tamīm.[54] Under these circumstances, it is difficult to determine whether Abū Bakr authorized the attack on Tamīm or not. But on the other hand, there is no indication to the effect that Abū Bakr objected to Khālid's conduct of the war and his resolution to attack Tamīm. On the contrary, Abū Bakr is always presented in the sources as giving his full support and encouragement to Khālid and, if anything, pleased and appreciative of this commander's exploits rather than critical and disappointed in him.

The tradition preserved many of the complaints about Khālid and about his conduct of the war. Also, it presents 'Umar as the arch-enemy of Khālid and the leader of a religiously oriented group who kept complaining about Khālid's behavior and urging the caliph to discharge him from his duties and to inflict upon him the appropriate penalties for the crimes he had committed. With regard to al-Buṭāḥ only, 'Umar and his group lodged three complaints against Khālid,

[52]Ṭab., I, 1880.
[53]Bal. *Fut.*, I, 114-118.
[54]Diyārbakrī, II, 209.

each one of which, according to Islamic law, carries the death penalty. In the first place, they alleged that Khālid, by ordering the execution of Mālik, committed the murder of a Muslim and should be put to death in retaliation.[55] This allegation was based on the grounds that Mālik was a Muslim, an agent of the prophet, and had not apostatized. Secondly, Khālid was accused of adultery. The plaintiffs alleged that Khālid married the wife of Mālik and consummated that marriage before the lapse of her ʿ*iddah* (three month period); and, therefore, he should be put to death by stoning.[56] Thirdly, the group protested against Khālid's treatment of the subjugated tribes. He is reported to have burned and tortured to death some "apostates" apparently to intimidate the tribes,[57] an act which was regarded as unlawful by that religious group. In all these cases, ʿUmar was the prosecutor and Abū Bakr the defender and supporter of Khālid. To those critics of Khālid, the caliph reportedly replied: "I would not sheathe a sword which God drew on the infidels."[58]

But even with the backing of Abū Bakr and the supporters of his policy, Khālid could not have marched on the territory of Tamīm without a reasonably sizeable army, especially when the Anṣār refused to join with him. Where did Khālid recruit his army? Were Sayf's report to be accepted, that Abū Bakr dispatched eleven armies at the same time, then Khālid would have departed from Dhū al-Qaṣṣah with a relatively small army. As has been pointed out above, only a portion of what the Muslims could have recruited went with Usāmah in his campaign to the Syrian border. After the departure of Usāmah and most likely before his return, Abū Bakr called

[55]Ṭab., I, 1926, 1928; Wathīmah, 12; *Aghānī*, XV, 242, 244; Diyārbakrī, II, 209.

[56]Ṭab., I, 1928-29; Ibn al-Athīr, II, 359; *Aghānī*, XV, 239; Wathīmah, 12; Baghdādī, *Khizānah*, I, 238; Diyārbakrī, II, 209.

[57]Bal. *Fut.*, I, 116; Ṭab., I, 1900.

[58]See notes 42, 43, and 44 above.

[59]Diyārbakrī, II, 204; see also Athīr, II, 351.

on the loyal tribes in the surroundings of Medina—Aslam, Ghifar, Musaynah, Ashja', Juhaynah, and Ka'b—to send contingents to help him fight the "apostates." These tribes were reported to have responded; and, evidently, their contingents constituted the Muslim army which Abū Bakr headed at Dhū al-Qaṣṣah. Before the battle of al-Buzākhah, Khālid, as was said above, detached the tribe of Ṭayyi' from the camp of the allied forces of Najd. With Ṭayyi' on his side, Khālid fought the battle of al-Buzākhah and won a victory over Ṭalḥah and his allies. After the battle, Khālid is reported to have stripped the defeated tribes of their arms and distributed these among those of his followers who were in need of them to fight the enemy.[60] Unfortunately, Diyārbakrī does not elaborate further and does not say who were those in need of arms. A report of Sayf, on the other hand, affirms that Abū Bakr ordered his commanders to recruit contingents from the tribes who remained loyal to Islam.[61] By "loyal to Islam," Sayf probably meant those tribes who did not take to arms against the Muslim army, and, most likely, he had in mind his own tribe, Tamīm. In another report, Sayf claims that a chief from Tamīm was sent by Khālid against the tribe of 'Amir b. Ṣa'ṣa'ah, after al-Buzākhah.[62] It is probably at this point, immediately following al-Buzākhah, that the chiefs of Tamīm started to join the Muslim army.

'Aqrabā'

'Aqrabā' is the name of the plain where, in bloody battle, the Muslim army under the command of Khālid b. al-Walīd fought Banū Ḥanīfah under the command of Musaylimah. Caetani places this battle at the end of year 11 or beginning of year 12.[63] From its description in the sources and the large

[60]Diyārbakrī, II, 208.
[61]Ṭabarī, I, 1880.
[62]Ṭabarī, I, 1899.
[63]Caetani, *Annali*, II/I, 558.

numbers of Muslims reported killed in it, 'Aqrabā' seems to have been the fiercest battle the Muslims saw in Arabia.[64] They won the final victory, however, and Musaylimah and the last of his followers were forced to seek refuge in a walled orchard, where reportedly they were all killed. This event is known in the history of Islam as *Ḥadīqat al-Mawt*, Garden of Death, because of the large number of people killed in it.[65] After the death of Musaylimah, Banū Ḥanīfah surrendered and concluded a peace treaty with Khālid.[66]

So far, the traditional sources are more or less agreed on the broad lines of the story of this battle. They are in disagreement, however, with regard to details which carry significant implications for the Riddah as a whole and the factional antagonisms in the Muslim camp. The controversy evolves around the question of the origin of the fighting with Banū Ḥanīfah, the objection of the Anṣār to carrying on the war under Khālid, and, as with previous battles, the conduct of Khālid himself. To attack a strong and stubborn foe—as the sources present Banū Ḥanīfah—one would expect the Muslims to assemble all their forces and launch them into battle. But apparently this was not the case. Evidence derived from the sources points in the other direction, i.e., only part of what the Muslims were able to recruit for their army was engaged against Banū Ḥanīfah; at the same time others were fighting elsewhere in Arabia or in the Syrian desert.

With regard to 'Aqrabā', Sayf presents the following story: From Dhū al-Qaṣṣah, Abū Bakr dispatched 'Ikrimah b. Abī Jahl, one of the eleven commanders, against Banū Ḥanīfah. The caliph also reinforced 'Ikrimah with an army under Shuraḥbīl; 'Ikrimah rushed head-long into battle against Banū Ḥanīfah, who inflicted on him a disastrous defeat. When the

[64]Ya'qūbi, II, 130; Bal. *Fut.*. Im 106, 108; Ṭab., I, 1942; Athīr, II, 363; Diyārbakrī, II, 212.

[65]Bal. *Fut.*, I, 107; Ṭab., I, 1943; Athīr, II, 364; Diyārbakrī, II, 215-217.

[66]Bal. *Fut.*, I, 108; Ṭab., I, 1951; Athīr, II, 365, Diyārbakrī, II, 218.

news of this defeat reached the caliph, he, indignant at the behavior of 'Ikrimah, ordered him to proceed south-east, join with Ḥudhayfah and 'Arfajah, and help them fight the people of 'Umān and Mahrah. Once 'Umān and Mahrah were subjugated, the order continues, 'Ikrimah should leave with his army and march to Ḥaḍramawt and Yemen, where he would join with al-Muhājir b. Abī Umayyah.[67] This was the route which 'Ikrimah in fact followed; whether he had received detailed orders from the caliph to do so, as Sayf claims, or not, and whether 'Ikrimah was sent on this mission as a punishment, as Sayf claims, or not, are disputable questions.

No other available source supports Sayf concerning 'Ikrimah's attack on Banū Ḥanīfah and the defeat he suffered at their hands. But a partial confirmation of Sayf's report is found in al-Ya'qūbī. The latter reports that the caliph dispatched Shuraḥbīl against Banū Ḥanīfah and later reinforced him with Khālid b. al-Walīd.[68] Ya'qūbī, however, does not mention any engagement with Banū Ḥanīfah before the arrival of Khālid; while Sayf claims that Shuraḥbīl, also, did the same as 'Ikrimah and met with the same results.[69] Thus, according to Sayf, there were two unsuccessful engagements with Banū Ḥanīfah previous to the arrival of Khālid at 'Aqrabā' where the decisive battle against Musaylimah took place. The other available sources do not mention either 'Ikrimah or Shuraḥbīl in connection with al-Yamāmah, nor do they speak of any fighting with Banū Ḥanīfah before the arrival of Khālid. Balādhurī says that Khālid, after having subjugated Najd in a few months, was sent by the caliph against Musaylimah.[70] Diyārbakrī, probably on the authority of al-Wāqidī, says that the caliph had ordered Khālid to march on Banū Ḥanīfah when, at Dhū al-Qaṣṣah, Khālid

[67] Ṭab., I, 1929; Athīr, II, 36.
[68] Ya'qūbī, II, 130.
[69] Ṭab., I, 1931.
[70] Bal. *Fut.*, I, 106.

was entrusted with the command of the Muslim army. The caliph insisted to Khālid that he should attack Banū Ḥanīfah once he had quelled the Riddah in al-Buzākhah.[71] Under these circumstances, one has either to reject Sayf or to reconcile him with others, hypothetically, in that a minor skirmish between Banū Ḥanīfah and ʻIkrimah might have taken place while ʻIkrimah was the agent of the prophet to Hawāzin, the neighbors of Banū Ḥanīfah.[72] Muslim traditionists disregarded these skirmishes, while Sayf, whose fondness for detail is characteristic of his reportage, gave the story in full colors with some commentary of his own.

Whatever the true case might have been, all sources agree that ʻIkrimah was not present at the battle of ʻAqtabā', while Shuraḥbīl, according to Sayf and al-Yaʻqūbī, was in Khālid's vanguard in that battle.[73] It is interesting to note that none of the prominent commanders of the Muslim army during both the Riddah and the conquest other than Shuraḥbīl is reported to have been with Khālid in al-Yamāmah. If this were true, then the question is: where were such people as ʻAmr b. al-ʻAṣ, Khālid b. Saʻīd, al-Muhājir b. Abī Umayyah, ʻIkrimah b. Abī Jahl, etc.? Were they fighting elsewhere? In that case, where? And where did they recruit their armies? These questions will be dealt with later in this chapter; but the immediate question in relation to ʻAqrabā' is: where did Khālid himself recruit an army large enough to encounter Banū Ḥanīfah and win a victory over them?

With regard to Khālid's army in ʻAqrabā', the tradition unfortunately gives only sketchy information. They speak of a large army under Khālid, but they do not specify further. A few remarks, scattered here and there in the sources, hint at the composition of that army.[74] From this scanty information it is learned that the army of Khālid at ʻAqrabā' was composed

[71]Diyārbakrī, II, 209.
[72]Ibn Ḥajar, *Iṣābah*, II, 489; Ibn ʻAbd al-Barr, *Istīʻāb*, 1082.
[73]Ṭab., I, 1938.
[74]Ṭab., I, 1930; Athīr, II, 363; Diyārbakrī, II, 160, 209.

of Muhājirun, Anṣār, and tribesmen. The tradition speaks of recrimination between the bedouins and the town dwellers in that army during the battle. Each side accused the other of cowardice and blamed it for the retreat in the face of the fierce charge of Banū Ḥanīfah.[75] It is evident that in the Muslim army under Khālid there were Medinans who were either Muhājirun or Anṣār; the problem, however, is to determine which bedouin tribes participated in that battle.

Diyārbakri reports that Abū Bakr, after the battle of al-Buzākhah, accepted the allegiance of the defeated tribes on the condition that they send contingents to Yamāmah to help Khālid fight Banū Ḥanīfah. "Safe is the one about whom Khālid writes to me that he attended Yamāmah with him! Let the present inform the absent! Don't come back to me! But make your way to Khālid!"—Abū Bakr is reported to have said to those tribes.[76] The lists of names of those who were killed in 'Aqrabā' as presented in the available sources include only names of Muhājirun and Anṣār; those of the tribesmen were disregarded.[77] But these sources speak of a relatively large number of bedouins killed in the battle.[78] Scattered references in the sources indicate that the tribes of Najd participated in 'Aqrabā' on the Muslim side. In a report by al-Diyārbakrī, the bedouins from Najd, Ghaṭafān, Asad, Tamīm, and Ṭayyi' were blamed for the retreat of the Muslims three times during the battle.[79] In another account, the same author gives a report on the authority of a man from Fazārah who claimed to have fought the Muslims in al-Buzākhah. After the battle, he came to surrender to Abū Bakr; the latter ordered him to go and join with Khālid in

[75]Ṭab., I, 1946-47; Athīr, II, 363; Diyārbakrī, II, 209, 212, 215.
[76]Diyārbakrī, II, 209.
[77]Athīr, II, 366-67; Dhahabī, Tarīkh, I, 364-472; Caetani, *Annali*, II/II, 739-754.
[78]Ṭab., I, 1946-47, 1951; Athīr, II, 365; Diyārbakrī, II, 219.
[79]Diyārbakrī, II, 209.

al-Yamāmah.[80] This information adds to what has been said above: that the defeated tribes were recruited into the Muslim army and with their help the Muslims furthered the war.

Here again as in the previous battles, the traditionists speak of the Anṣār's objection to participating in the war under Khālid and of the complaints regarding Khālid's conduct. Balādhurī reports that the Anṣār first refused to go along with Khālid's resolution to attack Banū Ḥanīfah but later regretted and joined with him.[81] After victory in the battle field, Khālid, having lost many of his men in the battle, concluded peace with Banū Ḥanīfah on the condition that they surrender their castles and pay tribute worth half of what they possessed. Khālid also married the daughter of Mujjā'ah, a chief from Banū Ḥanīfah, who negotiated the peace treaty with Khālid. According to Sayf, Abū Bakr wrote Khālid ordering him to kill every man who had come of age in Banū Ḥanīfah. But this letter reached Khālid only after he had concluded the peace treaty with them, therefore he kept his word to them and carried out his agreement.[82] The Anṣār, however, refused to accept the terms of the treaty and demanded that Abū Bakr's alleged orders be executed; still, Khālid refused to break his agreement. The Anṣār, having won in the main battle at 'Aqrabā', wanted to continue fighting, to storm the castles of Banū Ḥanīfah and to treat them as an enemy defeated by force. Khālid on the other hand, saw the difficulty of achieving what the Anṣār wanted especially after having lost so many of his army on the battlefield, and he favored a negotiated peace. The Anṣār probably suspected his conduct because of his marriage to the daughter of Mujjā'ah, and they saw the whole agreement as a sell-out depriving them of the fruits of their victory.[83] The Anṣār protested bitterly against Khālid's defiance of the caliph's

[80]Diyārbakrī, II, 209.
[81]Bal. *Fut.*, I, 107.
[82]Ṭab., I, 1955.
[83]Diyārbakrī, II, 218, 219.

orders and against his marriage to Mujjā'ah's daughter, especially at a time when Medinans had suffered so many casualties. And 'Umar and his group seconded the Anṣār in making these same protests against Khālid. Abū Bakr is reported to have reproached Khālid for these things but finally accepted Khālid's excuse and refused to bend to 'Umar's demands that Khālid be removed from the command of the army.[84]

Baḥrayn

The story of the war in Baḥrayn, as presented in the major traditional sources, is more of a legend than historical narrative. The historical information supplied in these sources is lost in long tales of miraculous events which supposedly happened to the Muslim army in Baḥrayn and on the way there.[85] Unlike other places in Arabia, the war in Baḥrayn lasted for a long time and was not a matter of a single decisive battle. In fact, the conquest of Baḥrayn was not completely accomplished until the time of 'Umar in the year 13.[86] As far as the war in Baḥrayn is concerned, the traditional sources hardly agree on anything other than that al-'Alā' b. al-Ḥaḍramī was the commander of the Muslim army there. Who sent al-'Alā' and when? Where did al-'Alā' recruit his army? Did Khālid b. al-Walīd go to Baḥrayn to reinforce al-'Alā' or not? Was the war in Baḥrayn going on simultaneously with that in other places? These are all questions to which the various sources give different answers. Under the circumstances, a consistent story based on all the available information and congruous with the historical background of the state of affairs in that area, as described in the previous chapters can be construed only tentatively.

[84]Diyārbakrī, II, 219; Ya'qūbī, II, 131.

[85]Ṭab., I, 1958-1975; Athīr, II, 368-372; cf. also Caetani, *Annali*, II/II, 774-76; Wellhausen, *Skizzen*, VI, 22-24.

[86]Bal. *Fut.*, I, 103; cf. also Caetani, *Annali*, II/II, 762-63.

Balādhurī, who eliminates all the legendary elements of the story, supplies the following information.[87] Following the death of the prophet, the people of Baḥrayn asked Abū Bakr to send al-Alā' back to Baḥrayn as agent; Abū Bakr honored their request. Except for al-Jarūd and his tribe, 'Abd al-Qays, all the people of Baḥrayn apostatized after the death of al-Mundhir b. Sāwā, "king" of Baḥrayn; this occurred shortly after the death of the prophet. The apostates designated a descendant of the kings of Ḥīrah as emir of Baḥrayn. When this news reached al-'Alā', he marched against the apostates and fought them. After this engagement, the defeated Muslims were forced to seek refuge in the castle of Juwāthah, a town in Baḥrayn. Finally, al-'Alā' staged a surprise attack on the besiegers and was victorious over them. In another account al-Balādhurī reports that some traditionists say al-'Alā' wrote to Abū Bakr informing him about the situation and asked for help. Abū Bakr wrote to Khālid ordering him to hurry to the aid of al-'Alā'. Khālid, however, arrived after al-Ḥuṭam, the leader of the apostates, was killed and together with al-'Alā' laid siege to al-Khaṭṭ, a town in Baḥrayn. At this point, Khālid received a letter from Abū Bakr with the orders to march to the Iraqi borders. Balādhurī observes that al-Wāqidī claimed Khālid went back to Medina from Yamāmah and from Medina set out for Iraq.

Ibn Isḥaq's version of the story, which was adopted by Caetani and used against Sayf's, says that Abū Bakr sent al-'Alā' to Baḥrayn only after the conquest of Yamāmah.[88] The continuation in *Majma' al-zawā'id* of this incomplete report, as given in Ṭabarī, adds that al-'Alā' was reinforced by Thumāmah b. Uthāl, the rival of Musaylimah among Banū Ḥanifah. The apostates besieged the Muslims in the castle of Juwāthah until they almost perished of starvation. At that point al-'Alā' staged the surprise night-attack on the

[87] Bal. *Fut.*, I, 99-103.

[88] Ṭab., I, 1959; Caetani, *Annali*, II/II, 771 (Nota 1).

apostates, defeated them, and dispersed them from around the castle.[89]

Sayf's story is more detailed and too picturesque to accept literally; but there is no reason to reject it outright as Caetani and Wellhausen did.[90] The essential points of this long story are the following:[91] Abū Bakr sent al-'Alā' against the apostates in Baḥrayn, presumably as one of the eleven commanders whom the caliph dispatched from Dhū al-Qaṣṣah. On his way to his destination, al-'Alā' was joined by Thumāmah b. Uthāl and, while passing through the land of Tamīm, this Muslim army was reinforced by as many warriors as it had originally numbered. These reinforcements came from al-Ribāb and 'Amr b. Tamīm, sections of Tamīm. On his arrival in Baḥrayn, al-'Alā' was joined by the tribe of 'Abd al-Qays. This army was strong enough to subdue al-Ḥuṭam and his followers from the tribe of Rabī'ah.[92]

So far, in all the battles which were fought in central Arabia, the name of al-'Alā' was not mentioned; and it is most likely that he was not with Khālid in al-Yamāmah. On the background of the movement in Baḥrayn, a hypothesis which might reconcile the various reports on al-'Alā's mission in Baḥrayn might be as follows: the tribes in Baḥrayn revolted against al-Mundhir b. Sāwā, previously an agent of the Persians and newly the ally of Muḥammad. Shortly after Muḥammad died, al-Mundhir died and his party was overwhelmed by the rebels. Al-Mundhir's adherents sought the help of Abū Bakr, who under the present circumstances could not afford to send a large army to relieve them. But, as al-Balādhurī and Sayf say, the caliph dispatched al-'Alā', most likely with a small army if any, as token of support. In Bahrayn, al-'Alā' was overridden by his enemies and was

[89]al-Haythamī ('Alī b. Abī Bakr), *Majma' al-zawā'id wa-manba' al-fawā'id*, VI, 220-221.

[90]Caetani, Annali, II/II, 772; Wellhausen, *Skizzen*, VI, 24.

[91]Ṭab., I, 1961-1975.

[92]Cf. also Athīr, II, 368-371.

besieged, apparently, for a long time. Some reports say al-'Alā' sought help from Abū Bakr, who could not supply it until after Musaylimah was defeated.

It is most unlikely that Khālid went to Baḥrayn himself, but it is possible that he sent some reinforcements to al-'Alā'. This might account for what Sayf claims regarding the tribes which joined al-'Alā' on his way to Baḥrayn. Al-'Alā' pursued the war against the towns of Baḥrayn while the rest of the Muslim commanders were fighting elsewhere. From the itinerary of Khālid's war activity, it is evident that he marched to the Iraqi borders and back to Syria before al-'Alā' achieved the complete submission of Baḥrayn.

'Umān and Mahrah

Caetani, following Ibn Isḥaq, dates the conquest of 'Umān and Mahrah in the first half of the year 12.[93] Others, however, claim that the whole war of al-Riddah happened during the year 11.[94]

As for 'Umān, the traditional sources are almost unanimous in delineating the course of events there. From these sources, it is understood that when the revolt against Medina's allies in 'Umān broke out, Abū Bakr sent Ḥudhayfah b. Miḥṣan to fight the rebels and later reinforced him with 'Ikrimah b. Abī Jahl. The two fought Laqīṭ, the head of the rebels, and defeated him. Ḥudhayfah remained as agent of Medina in 'Umān, 'Arfajah returned with the booty to Medina, and 'Ikrimah continued his march to Mahrah and Yemen.[95] According to Sayf, it was at the request of Medina's allies that Abū Bakr dispatched the armies to 'Umān.[96]

As regards Ḥudhayfah, the available sources do not supply

[93] Ṭab., I, 1976; Caetani, *Annali*, II/I, 561.

[94] Ṭab., I, 1976.

[95] Bal. *Fut.*, I, 92-93; Ṭab., I, 1977-1980; Athīr, II, 372-73; Caetani, *Annali*, II/II, 776-67.

[96] Ṭab., I, 1977.

information as to where he recruited his army and it is most likely that he had to rely on locally recruited forces from 'Umān. But, concerning 'Ikrimah, a report by Wāqidī supplies the information that 'Ikrimah went to 'Umān with an army from the tribe of Ka'b b. Rabī'ah.[97] This report supports the hypothesis made about 'Ikrimah's participation in the war against Banū Ḥanīfah and fits exactly with the other reports concerning 'Ikrimah's participation in the war of al-Riddah. From other sources it is learned that the prophet, in the year of his death, sent 'Ikrimah as his agent to the tribe of Hawāzin.[98] The tribe of Ka'b b. Rabī'ah, mentioned in Wāqidī's report, is a branch of Hawāzin,[99] and their dwellings to the south-east of Ṭā'if were the closest among the Muslim tribes to both Yamāmah and 'Umān. Due to this geographical factor, it seems the most reasonable thing for Abū Bakr to do, had he wanted to send an army to 'Umān, would have been to entrust 'Ikrimah with that mission. If 'Ikrimah were to rely on locally recruited men and not have any military support from Medina, there would have been no reason for his waiting until after Khālid's conquest of Najd. With his own army, 'Ikrimah could function independently in 'Umān—and simultaneously with Khālid's military activity in Najd.

It is possible that 'Ikrimah, while being an agent to Hawazin and before his departure to 'Umān, was ordered by the caliph to stage several attacks on Banū Ḥanīfah—to help the distressed minority which had allied itself with Medina against Musaylimah's followers. In his strategic location, 'Ikrimah could keep Banū Ḥanīfah busy defending their territory and prevent them from extending any help to the enemies of Medina in Najd. It seems also possible that Sayf's reports concerning 'Ikrimah's engagements with Banū Ḥanīfah refer to these skirmishes; other traditionists disregarded them. In

[97] Caetani, *Annali*, II/II, 776.
[98] Ibn Ḥajar, *Iṣābah*, II, 489; Ibn 'Abd al-Barr, III, 1082.
[99] Kaḥḥalah, *Mu'jam*, 984.

any event, it is evident that 'Ikrimah was not, as Sayf claims, dispatched with an army from Dhū al-Qaṣṣah; rather, in his capacity as agent of Medina to Hawāzin, he was entrusted with the command of an army that was assigned to 'Umān. It is also most doubtful that 'Ikrimah, as Sayf claims, was sent to 'Umān as punishment for his rash conduct in the war. It is most likely that the caliph ordered 'Ikrimah to march to 'Umān after Khālid's victory in al-Buzākhah and that an army large enough to invade Yamāmah was recruited from Ḥijāz and Najd.

From 'Umān, 'Ikrimah marched to Mahrah at the head of an army whose ranks were filled from the tribes in the conquered areas. There he sided with one chief, Shikhrit, against another, al-Muṣabbaḥ. The two defeated al-Muṣabbaḥ and his tribe, Muḥārib, and Mahrah submitted to Islam.[100] 'Ikrimah continued on his way to Yemen through Ḥadramawt, where he met with Ziyād b. Labīd and al-Muhājir b. Abī Umayyad; together they fought and subdued Kindah.[101]

Yemen

After al-Aswad's death, hostilities broke out amongst those who conspired against him and had suceeded in eliminating him. According to Sayf, apostasy broke out again in Yemen after the death of the prophet. This was, as Sayf calls it, the second Riddah.[102] Balādhurī, however, does not speak of another Riddah in Yemen. He only says that Qays b. Makshūḥ was accused of murdering Dadhawayh, the chief of the Abnā', and was scheming to drive the rest out of Yemen. When Qays surrendered to the Muslim commander in Ṣan'ā', the latter sent him to Abū Bakr. In Medina Qays swore that he had not killed Dādhawayh, and Abū Bakr released him.[103]

[100]Ṭab., I, 1980-81.
[101]Ṭab., I, 2001.
[102]Ṭab., I, 1989; Athīr, II, 375.
[103]Bal. *Fut.*, I, 127.

Also, al-Wāqidī does not speak of another Riddah in Yemen after al-Aswad's death.[104]

Elsewhere above, it has been said that the Muslim historians in general, and Sayf in particular, applied the term *Riddah* to wars in Arabia without justification. In his reports on Yemen, Sayf is a prime example of negligence. He speaks of second Riddah and goes on to narrate the following story: When Abū Bakr was elected caliph, he appointed Fayrūz as emir in Yemen. When Qays learned about that, he tried to rally the Yemeni Arabs around him and, with their help, to drive the foreign Abnā' from Yemen. The chiefs whom Qays contacted refused to extend any help to him and preferred to be neutral with regard to this conflict. Qays succeeded, however, in rallying the remnants of the army of al-Aswad around him and in forcing the Abnā' out of Ṣan'ā'. Fayrūz eventually succeeded in recruiting help from the tribes around Ṣan'ā', fought Qays, and defeated him.[105] In all of this, the Muslims were not a party. All this was evidently the continuation of the struggle for power in Ṣan'ā'. But Sayf chose to call it Riddah.

In another report, Sayf confirms al-Balādhurī in that Qays surrendered to the Muslim commander and was sent to Abū Bakr, who pardoned him.[106] This also indicates that the movement in Yemen was not directed against Medina: it was a local struggle in which every participant would have been only too happy to get the support of Medina. But each party seems to have been willing to try its chances at achieving its goals by force, in case Medinan support was granted to the others.

Sayf's reports on the war in Yemen indicate an example of how the Muslims carried out the war in Arabia. Confirmed by others, he reports that Abū Bakr sent al-Muhājir b. Abī

[104]Caetani, *Annali*, II/II, 791.
[105]Ṭab., I, 1990-93.
[106]Ṭab., I, 1998.

Umayyah to subdue Yemen.[107] Al Muhājir made his way through Mecca, where he was joined by an army under the command of Khālid b. Asīd, brother of the governor of Mecca. From Mecca, al-Muhājir proceeded on his way to Yemen through Ṭā'if, through the territory of Bajīlah, Najrān, and Yemen. In each one of these places, he was reinforced by another detachment.[108] From this report, it seems that al-Muhājir recruited his army from friendly tribes as he proceeded to his destination. If so, al-Muhājir, like 'Ikrimah, did not have to wait until the war in Najd had ended; having to recruit his army from tribes outside Najd, he could function independently from and simultaneously with the other commanders.

* * *

So far, the survey of the way has covered the activities of seven of the eleven commanders mentioned in the report of Sayf as having been dispatched against the apostatizing tribes. Out of the remaining four, two (Ṭurayfah b. Ḥājizah and Suwayd b. al-Muqarrin) played only minor roles in this war. But the other two, Khālid b. Sa'īd and 'Amr b. al-'Aṣ, were key figures in the history of early Islam. Their role in the war is of prime importance as far as the Riddah and the conquest movement—and the relation between them—are concerned.

Ṭurayfah was the brother of Ma'n b. Ḥājizah, who was the agent of Medina to a portion of his tribe, Sulaym. Ma'n led a contingent from his tribe to join with Khālid b. al-Walīd in the battle of al-Buzākhah and left his brother in charge of affairs among Sulaym. It seems to be at this point that a movement against Medina, led by one al-Fujā'ah, was touched off in a portion of Sulaym. Al-Fujā'ah, whose full name was Iyās b. 'Abd Yālīl, is reported to have come to Abū Bakr after the

[107]Ya'qūbī, II, 132; Bal. *Fut.*, I, 127; Ṭab., I, 1998; Athīr, II, 337; Caetani, *Annali*, II/II, 789.

[108]Ṭab., I, 1998; Athīr, II, 377.

break out of al-Riddah and to have offered his services to the Muslim state, if Abū Bakr could only supply him with the necessary arms; the caliph did. But, when al-Fujā'ah was back in his tribe, he turned against the Muslims in that area and began raiding the allies of Medina from Sulaym, 'Amir, and Hawāzin. Abū Bakr, therefore, ordered Ṭurayfah to fight him; Ṭurayfah did, succeeded in capturing him, and sent him to Abū Bakr in Medina, who, reportedly, had him burned alive. This is the only military activity Ṭurayfah is accredited with during the war of al-Riddah.[109]

Much less significant was the role played by Suwayd b. al-Muqarrin. No other source, except for Sayf, mentions his name. Even Sayf himself does not supply any additional information concerning Suwayd's activity in the war other than that he was sent by Abū Bakr to Tihāmah, the coastal region of Yemen. It seems that he played such an insignificant part in the war that it has not even been recorded.

As regards 'Amr b. al-'Aṣ and Khālid b. Sa'īd and their military activity in southern Syria, the traditional sources are confusing and in many cases seem contradictory. In this respect, Sayf b. 'Umar's reports stand in flagrant contradiction to those of Ibn Isḥāq and al-Wāqidī.[110] According to Sayf, 'Amr b. al-'Aṣ and Khālid b. Sa'īd were dispatched to Syria at the same time that the other commanders were sent from Dhū al-Qaṣṣah against the apostates.[111] Balādhurī, without mentioning his authorities, says that Abū Bakr sent three Muslim armies to Syria in the year 13; that was only after the Riddah had been done away with.[112] Ibn Isḥāq says that Abū Bakr dispatched the armies to Syria after his return from the pilgrimage of the year 12, i.e., in the beginning of the

[109]Ṭab., I, 1903-04; Bal. *Fut.*, I, 127; Athīr, II, 350-51; Caetani, *Annali*, II/II, 789.

[110]Cf. also De Goeje, 27; Caetani, *Annali*, II/II, 1119-35; Wellhausen, Skizzen, VI, 52-68.

[111]Ṭab., I, 1880-81, 2080.

[112]Bal. *Fut.*, I, 128.

year 13.[113] Mūsā b. 'Uqbah and Wāqidī speak of the dispatch of three armies to Syria without giving any dates.[114] The sources are in disagreement as to who were their commanders, which was the first to depart, and who was the commander-in-chief of the whole Muslim army in Syria.[115]

Caetani locates the departure of the armies to Syria in the second half of the year 12. He made this conclusion on the basis of comparison between the different reports and a reconciliation of a report by Ibn Isḥāq and another by Ibn Sa'd.[116] If this view of Caetani is accepted, or the reports of Ibn Isḥāq and Balādhurī are deemed more reliable than those of Sayf, then it seems that one has to account for the question: what did these distinguished commanders, whose names are connected with the conquest of Syria, do during the almost two years between the death of the prophet and the end of the so-called war of al-Riddah. As has been pointed out, 'Amr b. al-'Aṣ was in 'Umān and Khālid b. Sa'īd in Yemen at the time of the prophet's death; the two returned to Medina immediately after that. There is no record of their being involved in the war in Arabia itself, and the sources which contradict Sayf (and on whom Caetani and Wellhausen base their arguments) do not supply information concerning the whereabouts of these two outstanding commanders during this period of time. Another problem remains to be solved if the reports of Sayf are to be rejected; and that is: who was responsible for the shift of the tribes in southern Syria from the Byzantine to the Muslim side.[117]

With regard to these questions, Ibn 'Asākir fortunately preserved in his *Tārīkh Dimashq* a large number of traditions representing several points of view. Following is a résumé of

[113]Ṭab., I, 2079; 'Asākir, I, 449.
[114]'Asākir, 446-48.
[115]Cf. De Geoje, 25.
[116]Caetani, *Annali*, II/II, 1121.
[117]Caetani, *Annali*, II/II, 1115.

Ibn 'Asākir's main reports, arranged according to his authorities.

(1) *Ibn Isḥāq.* The conquest of Yamāmah, Yemen, Baḥrayn, and the dispatch of the Muslim armies to Syria were all in the year 12.[118] When Abū Bakr was bent on attacking the Byzantines, he consulted with the prominent companions; they agreed with him and accepted his opinion. Abū Bakr, thereafter, urged the Muslims to participate in this campaign. Khālid b. Sa'īd was designated commander. But, before the departure of his army, the prominent companions inspected it and expressed their dissatisfaction with its equipment. Therefore, they advised Abū Bakr to write to the people of Yemen and urge them to take part in the campaign; Abū Bakr did.[119] As reported in Ibn 'Asākir, Ibn Isḥāq does not say whether this army went eventually to its destination or not.

(2) *Wāqidī.* When Abū Bakr decided to dispatch armies to conquer Syria, the first of his commanders to depart was 'Amr b. al-'Aṣ. He had three thousand men in his army.[120] Ibn Sa'd, Wāqidī's scribe, adds that Abū Bakr appointed 'Amr commander of all those tribes through whose territory 'Amr would pass: Balīy, 'Udhrah, and Quḍā'ah. The caliph ordered 'Amr to call the tribes for holy war, *jihād*, and that he should urge them to it, give riding beasts and equipment to those who followed him, and keep the tribes apart.[121]

(3) *Mūsā b. 'Uqbah.* When Abū Bakr was elected caliph, he dispatched three armies to Syria, the commanders of which were Khālid b. Sa'īd, 'Amr b. al-'Aṣ, and Shuraḥbīl b. Ḥasanah. The caliph however, under 'Umar's pressure, discharged Khālid b. Sa'īd and appointed Yazīd b. Abī Sufyān in his stead. The caliph also ordered Khālid b. al-Walīd to march to Syria after he had subjugated Yamāmah. Khālid, after a raid on 'Ayn al-Tamr and Dūmah, arrived in Syria and

[118] 'Asākir, 441.
[119] *Ibid.*, 433-45.
[120] *Ibid.*, 446.
[121] *Ibid.*

fought in the battle of Ajnadayn together with four other commanders. In Ajnadayn, the commanders were Abū 'Ubaydah b. al-Jarrāḥ, Yazīd b. Abī Sufyān, 'Amr b. al-'Āṣ, and Shuraḥbil b. Ḥasanah.[122] In this report Mūsā stands alone in contradiction of all other traditions in that he is the only one who says that Khālid was dispatched to Syria—but from a different direction.

(4) *Shuraḥbīl b. Marthad.* During his caliphate, Abū Bakr sent Khālid b. al-Walīd to Yamāmah and Yazīd b. Abī Sufyān to Syria. Abū 'Ubaydah asked 'Umar for reinforcement; the latter wrote to Khālid b. al-Walīd, who was already in Iraq, to march to Syria and help Abū 'Ubaydah.[123] The importance of this report—which seems to be a Syrian tradition—lies in the fact that it clearly states that Abū 'Ubaydah was sent to Syria by 'Umar and not by Abū Bakr.

(5) *Sayf b. 'Umar.* Abū Bakr dispatched Khālid b. Sa'īd to Syria at the same time that he sent Khālid b. al-Walīd to Iraq. In Syria, Khālid b. Sa'īd hurried to engage the Byzantines in battle; he was defeated, his son was killed, and he fled back to the desert. After his defeat, Khālid wrote to Abū Bakr informing him about the situation and asking for help. The caliph wrote to 'Amr b. al-'Āṣ, who was in the land of Quḍā'ah, ordering him to march and reinforce the Muslims there. Furthermore, Abū Bakr wrote to Khālid b. al-Walīd in Iraq to return to Syria and join with the Muslims in the war against the Byzantines.[124]

(6) *'Abd al-Raḥmān b. Jubayr.* After the Muslims, with the help of God, won a victory over the apostates and the infidels from Banū Ḥanīfah, Abū Bakr ordered Khālid b. al-Walīd to march to Iraq. Khālid departed with six thousand men. Then Abū Bakr prepared an army composed of Muhājirūn, Anṣār, newly converted Muslims from the subjugated tribes, and contingents from the Yemeni tribes. This army, the

[122] *Ibid.*, 448.
[123] *Ibid.*, 462.
[124] *Ibid.*, 463.

number of which is given as 24,000, was divided into four divisions; Abū 'Ubaydah, 'Amr b. al-'Aṣ, Shuraḥbil b. Ḥasanah, and Yazīd b. Abī Sufyān were commanders of the four divisions. Yazīd was the commander-in-chief.[125]

(7) *al-Zuhrī.* Abū Bakr sent an army under Khālid b. al-Walīd to Iraq; to Syria, the caliph dispatched three armies under the command of Khālid b. Sa'īd, Amr b. al-'Aṣ, and Shuraḥbīl b. Ḥasanah. 'Umar, however, insisted that Abū Bakr appoint Yazīd b. Abī Sufyān commander of an army; the caliph did.[126]

One way of resolving this complicated problem would be to reject some reports as unreliable, adopting certain versions of the story as more reasonable and acceptable—as some critical European scholars who have dealt with this problem have done.[127] There seems, however, to be another way of viewing these seemingly contradictory reports. Against the background of the achievements of the prophet in the north and the accounts of the course that the war in Syria was taking, these reports give a meaningful story—if they were viewed as complementary rather than contradictory. Furthermore, if the first alternative were followed, a question would arise which doesn't have a convincing answer, namely: according to what criteria are certain reports to be ruled out as unreliable? The Arab tribes in southern Syria were not brought under Muḥammad's control. In the accounts of the first battles in the conquest of Syria and Palestine, there is no record of fighting between the Muslims and those tribes. Traditional sources—as well as modern scholars—speak only of a war with the Byzantines.[128] Not only this, but, according to Theophane, the Muslim penetration into southern Syria was facilitated by and made possible through the co-operation

[125] *Ibid.*, 453.

[126] *Ibid.*, 453-54.

[127] Cf. Caetani, *Annali*, II/II, 1119-35; 1161-73.

[128] Bal. *Fut.*, I, 130; 'Asākir, 478-488; Caetani, *Annali*, II/II, 1176; De Goeje, 30, 31.

of the Arab tribes who settled in that area.[129] And the question here is: at whose hands did these Arab tribes shift positions from the Byzantine to the Muslim side and when?

It seems that the confusion in the sources emanated from mixing two issues: one is the Muslim engagement with the Arab tribes in southern Syria and the second is the war with the Byzantines. The controversy concerning the commanders and the commander-in-chief of the Muslim armies seems to have been caused by the numerous detachments, each under a different prominent companion, which were consecutively dispatched to Syria. If this thesis is accepted, then the traditional reports might fit in to give a meaningful story of the invasion of Syria and its relation to the war of al-Riddah. Furthermore, Sayf's reports would then he reconciled with those of al-Wāqidī, Ibn Isḥāq, and others.

From Sayf's report it is learned that the caliph sent 'Amr b. al-'Aṣ to Palestine, where the tribe of Quḍā'ah had settled, and Khālid b. Sa'īd to al-Balqā' in Jordan, where the tribe of Kalb had settled; at the same time other commanders were dispatched to other destinations in Arabia. There is no tangible reason to reject this report. On the contrary, it seems to be the most reasonable thing for the Muslims to have done. As has been pointed out above, simultaneously with Khālid b. al-Walīd's military activity in Najd, 'Ikrimah b. Abī Jahl led his troops to 'Umān, Mahrah, Ḥaḍramawt, and eventually to Yemen. At the same time, al-Muhājir b. Abī Umayyah proceeded from Medina to Mecca, Ṭā'if, and eventually to Yemen to meet with 'Ikrimah. Khālid recruited for his army the tribes who inhabited the area to the east and north-east of Medina, 'Ikrimah recruited the tribes to the south-east for his army, and al-Muhājir drew upon the tribes of the area to the south-west of Medina for an army. To the north and north-west of Medina were the tribes of 'Udhrah, Balīy, and parts of Quḍā'ah, who became Muslim or allied themselves

[129] De Goeje, 29.

with Medina during the prophet's lifetime. They did not apostatize, and there is no record of their participation in the war in Arabia itself. It seems to be most sensible, therefore, that Abū Bakr recruit these tribes and make use of their military power. Actually, the report of Ibn Sa'd states clearly that the caliph sent 'Amr to these tribes in the north-west and ordered him to recruit an army from amongst them. This report of Ibn Sa'd is, in a way, a partial confirmation of Sayf's.

Also, the selection of the two men, 'Amr and Khālid b. Sa'īd, for this difficult mission to the Byzantine borders speaks in favor of the acceptance of Sayf's account. 'Amr, one of the shrewdest figures of early Islam, had served on such a mission during the lifetime of the prophet—in 'Umān and among the tribes to the north-west of Medina. Because of his diplomatic abilities and the fact that his mother was from the tribe of Balīy, who had settled in that area, 'Amr was chosen for the mission.[130] The selection of Khālid b. Sa'īd was for no less significant reasons: being an Umayyad, whose clan's commercial relations had brought them into close aquaintance with the Arab tribes on the Byzantine borders and being one of the earliest converts to Islam, Khālid was an excellent choice for such a mission. Through diplomacy and threat of military action, the two commanders succeeded in detaching the Arab tribes from the Byzantine camp. Their success was facilitated by the short-sighted Byzantine policy towards their Arab auxiliaries who defended the borders of the empire against nomadic intrusion.[131] Abū Bakr was certainly aware of the situation among these tribes, and his choice of the two men for such a mission—which necessitated more diplomacy than power —was a master's stroke.

It was not until the task of winning the Arab tribes in southern Syria to the Muslim side was accomplished, and the

[130] *E. I.*, article " 'Amr b. al-'Aṣ" by A. J. Wensink.
[131] De Goeje, 29-30.

two together had to face a Greek Byzantine army, that 'Amr informed the caliph about the situation and asked for help. At this point Khālid b. al-Walīd had already defeated Banū Ḥanīfah and marched north-east through the Syrian Desert towards the borders of Iraq. Otherwise, the dispatch of Shuraḥbīl b. Ḥasanah to Syria, as is reported unanimously by traditionists, could not have been possible. Shuraḥbīl, as has been pointed out above, was the vanguard of Khālid b. al-Walīd in the battle of 'Aqrabā. And it seems that after the Muslim victory in Yamāmah, Shuraḥbīl returned to Medina and from there led his army to Syria, while Khālid marched to the Iraqi borders and from there back to Syria, as can be seen in the report earlier in this chapter attributed to Mūsā b. 'Uqbah.

In the second half of the year 12, as is reported by Ibn Isḥāq, Arabia was pacified, and the subjugated tribes were incorporated into the Muslim army and sent to Syria. Bedouin detachments organized on tribal lines and put under Muslim commanders, mainly from Quraysh, streamed from Medina to the front against the Byzantines.[132] It is most likely at this stage that Khālid b. Sa'īd was replaced by Yazīd b. Abī Sufyān, possibly because of Khālid's rash engagement in battle with the Byzantines. In this engagement, according to Sayf, Khālid was led into a trap by the Byzantines, his son was killed, and he retreated to the desert. Yazīd was probably the first among the commanders of the reinforcements to depart. This group was dispatched at the end of year 13 or beginning of 13. Its destination was the Jordan of today, where Khālid b. Sa'īd was dealt defeat at the hands of the Byzantines.[133] These armies joined with 'Amr b. al-'Aṣ, who was already in southern Palestine, in the battle of Ajnadayn.

In general, this survey of the war in Arabia and the subsequent invasion of the Syrian Desert confirms the report of

[132]Ya'qūbī, II, 133.

[133]Cf. also, Caetani, *Annali*, II/II, 1168.

Sayf b. 'Umar concerning the dispatch of eleven armies by Abū Bakr. It is obvious, however, that one does not have to take this report literally and assume that all these armies were first recruited and then dispatched on the same day, as the wording of the report infers. But, it is evident that this operation was carried out in a relatively short span of time. Sayf's understanding of the situation in Arabia after the death of the prophet seems to be quite sound, and his analysis of the course of events in that area, at that juncture of its history, seems to be quite reasonable. There is no tangible reason for dismissing him and considering his reports imaginary or forged historical narratives.[134]

* * *

Against the background of the conclusions arrived at in the previous chapter concerning the extent and character of the Riddah and the thesis presented in this chapter concerning the course of the war in Arabia and the Syrian Desert during the caliphate of Abū Bakr, it seems possible to draw the following six conclusions:

(1) The so-called War of al-Riddah and the Arab conquest movement are one and the same operation, aimed at speading the hegemony of Medina over all the Arabs in Arabia and the Syrian Desert as well. This operation ended in an encounter first with the Byzantines and then with the Persians, the two Big Powers of the time. The results of these encounters decided the future history of the Near and Middle East.

(2) The military operations of the first effort, i.e., the subjugation of the Arabs, were carried out simultaneously and in four different directions. In the east and northeast of Medina, Khālid b. al-Walīd, Shuraḥbīl b. Ḥasanah, and al-'Alā' b. al-Ḥaḍramī fought and defeated the tribes of Ṭayyi', Ghaṭafān, Asad, Tamīm, Banū Ḥanīfah, and Rabī'ah. In the southeast, 'Ikrimah b. Abī Jahl, Ḥudhayfah b. Miḥṣah, and 'Arfa-

[134]See Becker, *op. cit.*, 337.

jah b. Harthamah won over the tribes of 'Umān and Mahrah. In the south-west, al-Muhājir b. Abī Umayyah and Ziyād b. Labīd conquered Yemen and Ḥaḍramawt. In the north and north-west, 'Amr b. al-'Aṣ and Khālid b. Sa'īd succeeded in winning the tribes on the Byzantine border to the Muslim side.

(3) Except for Khālid b. al-Walīd, who departed with an army from Medina, all the rest recruited their armies from among friendly tribes on the way to their destinations. Khālid was entrusted with the command of the army that Abū Bakr assembled at Dhū alQaṣṣah. This factor, i.e., the fact that Khālid's army included Muhājirūn and Anṣār, contributed to the prominence of Khālid's war activity in the annals of the early years of Islam. But even with a Medinan army for a start, Khālid had to recruit other tribes on his way to his destination. With contingents from Ṭayyi', he fought Ghaṭafān and Asad in al-Buzākhah, and after this battle Tamīm surrendered and joined with Khālid's army. With recruitments from all the tribes to the north-east of Medina, Khālid fought and won the battle of 'Aqrabā'. Once Najd was conquered, he, with a chosen body of warriors, joined with al-Muthannā b. Ḥārithah, leader of Shaybān from Bakr b. Wā'il, in fighting the Arab tribes in the Syrian Desert on the Persian border. Khālid was not the only commander to recruit an army that way: 'Ikrimah b. Abī Jahl drew on Hawāzin for an army that subdued 'Umān and Mahrah, and proceeded to meet with al-Muhājir in Ḥaḍramawt. The army of al-Muhājir kept swelling with contingents recruited in each station on his way from Medina to Yemen. From Mecca, Ṭā'if, and the tribes in northern Yemen, al-Muhājir built the army with which he conquered Yemen and Ḥaḍramawt. 'Amr b. al-'Aṣ and Khālid b. Sa'īd drew on the tribes of the north and north-west of Medina for an army.

(4) By the time 'Amr b. al-'Aṣ won the Arabs in southern Syria to the Muslim side and they had to face a Byzantine army towards the end of the year 12/beginning of 13, Arabia

had been pacified and Khālid b. al-Walīd was on the borders of Iraq. At this point, 'Amr requested reinforcements from Abū Bakr, and the latter began to dispatch one detachment after another as the victorious Muslim commanders began to return to Medina from the different parts of Arabia. The front in Syria against the Byzantines was continuously re-inforced by fresh forces recruited from among the newly defeated tribes in Arabia. The caliph also ordered Khālid b. al-Walīd to return to Syria and join with the Muslim army there.

(5) It is a wrong notion to consider the attack on the Byzantine border in Syria or Ḥīrah on the Persian border as the starting point of the Arab conquest movement. The subjugation of the Arab tribes in the Syrian Desert, which borders on both Iraq and Syria and which was inhabited by Arabs in the service of either the Byzantines or the Persians, was part and parcel of the Medinan plan of spreading its hegemony over all the Arabs as a first step in the Muslim expansion. For the Medinan policy-makers there was no difference between Baḥrayn and Ḥīrah or Dūmat al-Jandal; they were all inhabited by Arabs and were well-known by the Meccan merchants for a long time. This first step in the expansion movement started immediately after the surrender of Mecca.

(6) Except in the battle of 'Aqrabā', where Banū Ḥanīfah fought fiercely in defense of their territory, the Muslims were met with weak resistance in conquering Arabia. This weakness of the Arab tribes in resisting the Muslims was due to internal as well as external factors. These factors will be dealt with in the following chapter.

5. THE SUCCESS OF ABU BAKR

DURING HIS CALIPHATE OF A LITTLE OVER TWO YEARS, the first caliph of Islam was able to score two significant achievements. One was the spread of the hegemony of Medina over all the Arabs in Arabia as well as over a sizeable portion of those tribes inhabiting the Syrian Desert. Under Abū Bakr, the Arabian peninsula became—for the first time in history—a political unit. Through the subjugation of all pockets of resistance to Islam by resolute commanders of the Medinan armies, the caliph established himself as the undisputed leader of all Arabians.

Abū Bakr's first achievement was to effect the victory of Islam over tribalism. The second was his organization of the Muslim armies' first thrust against the two great empires of the time—Byzantium and Persia. Muslim armies were able to overcome the two empires in a short time.

In the course of achieving this success, Abū Bakr had to surmount a number of internal difficulties as well as external ones. At home, in Medina, he had to overcome the opposition of the Anṣār without causing civil war and fraternal bloodshed. The Anṣār were opposed to Meccan domination of state affairs, and they tried hard to prevent it from happening; they failed, however, to secure the office of caliph for one of their number. It was in the rivalry between the aristocracy of Quraysh and the Anṣār for hegemony in the new Muslim state that Goldziher saw the formulation of tribal pride on the basis of their southern or northern descent. In his view, the Anṣār boasted of a southern background to counterbalance Quraysh's claims of nobility and prestige.[1] This antagonism between northern Qays and southern Yaman peoples persisted with devastating effects—even to modern times.

Abū Bakr had to carry out his policy in spite of strong opposition to it by a number of prominent companions. The group was headed by 'Umar. As to what 'Umar's policy was, the tradition does not supply much information. What one might gather is that 'Umar advocated a lenient policy towards the "apostates." It is highly unlikely that he was against expansion as such. Later events, especially during his caliphate are proof of his zeal for expansion. It is possible, however, that 'Umar opposed the change of policy towards the tribes introduced by the prophet after the surrender of Mecca. He probably felt the growing influence of the Meccan aristocracy on the prophet's policy and opposed it out of deep religious feeling. This might have also been the reason behind 'Umar's opposition to Abū Bakr himself. The latter followed the prophet's line of policy, evidently, with full Meccan support; and 'Umar carried over his opposition to that policy. Witnessing the clever Meccan merchants advancing to the forefront of the Muslim community, 'Umar and his group of early Muhājirūn, who thought themselves more entitled to prominence in that state, tried to prevent them from dominating the political scene in Medina and to keep them away from running the state's affairs.

Outside Medina and the Ḥijāz, Abū Bakr had to face those several movements in Arabia which were known as al-Riddah. These movements—whether motivated by hostility to centralism, by aspiration to create a set-up similar to that of Medina,

[1]Ignaz Goldziher, *Muslim Studies* (tr. by C.R. Barber & S.M. Stern, Chicago, 1966), 90-91.

or in order to preserve local heritage and *status quo*—were all antagonistic to Medina's policy of expanding its hegemony over all the Arabs. Muslim concern with the external front and their engagement in war with the tribes of Arabia soon overshadowed internal rivalries and forced the Muslims to consolidate their efforts so as to maintain their very existence. These internal antagonisms, however, kept smoldering until 'Uthman's times when they burst out into civil war. For the time being, however, Abū Bakr was successful in harnessing all Muslim energies to the task of engaging the non-Muslim Arabs and subjugating them to the authority of Medina.

The expansionist policy, which Abū Bakr inherited from the prophet and which was advocated by the Meccan aristocracy and supported by their nomadic allies, met with success in Arabia and in the Syrian Desert as well. Many theories have been posited regarding the factors contributing to the success of the Arab conquest movement.[2] Also, the reasons for the success of Muḥammad's policy have been studied and set forth by many historians of early Islam.[3] But, as far as the initial steps of Abū Bakr's war of expansion and its success are concerned, other *local* reasons played the more significant roles.

The infant Muslim state of Medina, in order to be able to achieve that which it did, should have had at least a relatively sizeable and organized body of devoted supporters who could function fast and exploit the situation, which existed at that time in Arabia, to the state's advantage. That body of supporters was, as has been pointed out, supplied by Meccans and their tribal allies. The task of subjugating Arabia to caliphal authority was facilitated by the existing circumstances in the various geo-political units of Arabia at the time.

* * *

[2]Bousquet, *loc. cit.*
[3]Watt, 142-50.

In Najd two battles decided the supremacy of Islam over that area. Al-Buzākhah brought Asad and Ghaṭafān under Muslim control, and the battle of 'Aqrabā' broke Banū Ḥanīfah's resistance to Medinan domination. It is interesting to note that Muslim sources emphasize the point that the tribes in both battles fought the Muslims under the command of so-called "false prophets." It seems the traditional tribal leadership and its customary ways of conducting their tribes' affairs both in peace and war, through alliances etc., were no match for the rising Muslim power and its leadership and, therefore, tribal leadership tried to follow the Muslim example. A series of "prophets" made their appearance at this point.

Al-Buzākhah was won with little effort. The allied forces of Asad and Ghaṭafān did not have sufficient power to repulse the Muslim attack, especially after the withdrawal of Ṭayyi' from the alliance. In addition, the allied tribes were faced, for the first time in their history, with a new kind of war. It was not a raid of the *ghazw* type, to which they were accustomed and towards which their warlike activities were geared. This was a war aimed at permanent subjugation. The protagonists were a people with a cause and far-reaching plans. Furthermore, the allies suffered from another weakness, which was a lack of competent leadership.

In comparison with Muḥammad, who furnished his community with a workable system of religious and political life, Ṭalḥah, the leader of the allies at al-Buzākhah and whom Muslim sources declare a "false prophet," had nothing of the sort to offer his followers to counter Muḥammad's attractive call. If Ṭalḥah ever made the claim to prophethood, we are, for lack of information, far from able to form any idea about his teachings. From the very scanty data in the sources regarding his prophecies, he seems to have been a soothsayer rather than a prophet. Had Ṭalḥah wanted to ride the wave of enthusiasm for prophets which pervaded the peninsula at the time, he certainly came too late to establish his leadership and rally enough loyal support to withstand the Muslim onslaught. The alliance which he hurriedly put together crumbled at the first encounter with Khālid ibn al-Walīd and his Muslim army.

The career of the "false prophetess" and soothsayer, Sajāḥ, is even more ambiguous and distorted in the sources than that of Ṭalḥah. She made her appearance at the same time in the tribe of Tamīm, causing further frictions between the various groups of that tribe and eventually bringing disaster upon her supporters, Banū Yarbū'. It seems Musaylimah regarded alliance with her forces more a burden than an advantage and, therefore, he made sure to have them out of his territory before the decisive encounter with the Muslims. Whatever the prophetic message of Sajāḥ and her relations with Musaylimah, they definitely were not a great help to Tamīm. Tamīm was easily taken over by the Muslim army.

In the battle of 'Aqrabā', Banū Ḥanīfah were overwhelmed by an army which comprised contingents from almost all the tribes of the Ḥijāz and Najd plus parts of Tamīm. Banū Ḥanīfah stood fast against the Muslim invasion and fought a bloody battle, the likes of which the Muslims had not witnessed on Arabian soil. But, overwhelmed and outnumbered by their invaders, Banū Ḥanīfah were defeated and paid dearly for their determination to stand in the way of Muslim expansion. Among other factors which contributed to the defeat of Banū Ḥanīfah, two were major: the death of the prestigious Hawdhah ibn 'Alī, former "king" of Yamāmah; and the lack of support by the Persians to their agent in that area. Hawdhah's death was followed by a split in the ranks of Banū Ḥanīfah, and a splinter group of them joined forces with the invading Muslim army. No less important in determining the result of the confrontation with Islam was the character of Musaylimah's movement.

Musaylimah attempted to devise a viable religious and social system for his followers, but our primary sources supply very little reliable data on the specifics of his teachings. His mission was, possibly, a reaction to that of Muḥammad.[4] The fervor with which the followers of Musaylimah fought the Muslims may be partially attributed to the religious aspect of his leadership. But it was his movement's appeal to local patriotism and tribal solidarity which held his men together in resisting a superior force. Musaylimah's movement aimed at establishing an independent principality in Yamāmah along the traditional tribal pattern. He tried to resist assimilation in the supra-tribal Islamic movement and to confront Muḥammad's challenge with a fusion of prophethood and tribal solidarity. Musaylimah's attempt was unsuccessful, and its failure bears witness to the strength of Islam and the responsiveness of its ideology to the needs of the Arabian society at the time.

The eastern coast of Arabia was inhabited by Arabs who, at this juncture of their history, were under Persian rule. Persians regarded the inhabitants of Baḥrayn and 'Umān as rivals in trade with the East; the Persians therefore had extended their rule over these areas in order to control trade activities in them.[5] In the heyday of the city of al-Ḥīrah, these eastern localities were under the aegis of the Lakhmid kings. But once the kingdom of al-Ḥīrah was ruined and the ruling Lakhmid dynasty exterminated, the chiefs of eastern Arabia became the direct agents of the Persians in their localities thus gaining greater prominence. Ibn Ḥabīb, in his *al-Muḥabbar*, imparts the following passage concerning the fair of al-Mushaqqar in Baḥrayn:

> Then they [the merchants] set out from it [Dūmat al-Jandal] to al-Mushaqqar in Hajar. This fair was held from the beginning of Jumādā I until its end. Persians used to cross the sea and come to it with their merchan-

[4]*E. I.*, article "Musailima by Fr. Buhl; Wellhausen, *Skizzen*, VI, 17; see also Dale Eickelman, "Musaylimah," *JESHO*, X, 17-52.

[5]Irfan Kawar, "The Arabs in the peace treaty of A.D. 561," *Arabica* 3, 1957, pp. 181-213.

> dise; then they disperse till the same time of the following year. ʿAbd al-Qays and Tamīm were neighbors to this fair. Its kings were from Tamīm, from Banū ʿAbd Allah b. Zayd, the clan of al-Mundhir b. Sāwā. The Persian kings used to appoint them agents over the fair, as they appoint Banū Naṣr in al-Ḥirah, and Banū al-Mustakbir in ʿUmān. They [the Tamīmī kings] used to perform and behave in it the way the kings of Dūmat al-Jandal did and they used to levy the tithe from the merchants.[6]

In another passage concerning ʿUmān and Mahrah, Ibn Ḥabīb gives the following:

> Another fair was that of Ṣuḥār and ʿUmān. It was usually held on the first day of Rajab and lasted for five nights. Al-Julandā b. al-Mustakbir used to levy the tithe from the merchants there. Another fair was that of Dabbā. Dabbā is one of the two ports of the Arabs; merchants from Sind, India, China, people of the East and the West, came to it. This fair was held on the last day of Rajab. Merchants traded her by bargaining. Al-Julandā b. al-Mustakbir levied the tithe in this fair as in Ṣuḥār. He used to behave in it like other kings elsewhere. Another fair was that of al-Shiḥr—Shiḥr of Mahrah. It took place at the foot of the mountain on which the grave of the prophet Hūd is located. At this fair no tithes were levied because Mahrah was not a realm of a kingdom. Merchants coming to it took protection from Banū Muḥārib b. Harb of Mahrah. The fair of Shiḥr was held in the middle of Shaʿbān.[7]

The foregoing passages from Ibn Ḥabīb clearly point out Persian interest in the fairs of the eastern coast of Arabia. The Persians being badly in need of money to meet the high costs

[6] Ibn Ḥabīb, 265.
[7] *Ibid.*, 265-66.

of their war effort against the Byzantines,[8] extended their rule to this area by appointing local chiefs as their agents to these fairs so as to control trade efficiently there. The main function of agents in the trade centers of Arabia's eastern coast was to exact customs duties from merchants who had come to trade in the fairs and to submit these monies to the imperial treasury. As long as the Persian empire was strong and able to extend its active support to agents, their authority was not disputed and the Arab tribes yielded to their leadership. But once the Persians lost that ability, especially after the war of 622-628 A.D., in which they were defeated by Heracleus, their agents in Arabia were left on their own. It was only natural, therefore, that rival local chiefs challenge the authority of the agents. This had been the case, indeed, both in Baḥrayn and 'Umān. The conquest of these areas by the Muslims was facilitated by strife between local chiefs. With two antagonistic parties contending for control over the fairs in each of these localities, the Muslims were able to step in with only a small force—and *that* was enough to disturb the sensitive balance of power there and give the edge to that party which allied itself with Medina. In both Baḥrayn and 'Umān only a small force was needed to help whichever party was inclined to accept the hegemony of Medina to conquer its rivals. It is interesting to note that in both cases, in Baḥrayn as well as in 'Umān, the Muslims supported former agents of the Persians. Most likely these agents, knowing that their authority was deteriorating, turned to Medina in desperate quest of support to replace that of their former lords, the weakening Persians.

Al-Muhājir b. Abī Umayyah conquered Yemen almost without fighting. After a conquest by the Abyssinians, a reconquest with Persian help, the establishment of Persian rule in Yemen, and the dwindling of that rule because of lack of support from the center—there was chaos in the south-

[8]Irfan Kawar, *op. cit.*, 193.

western corner of the peninsula.[9] With the tribes divided among themselves, the rule of the Abnā' limited to Ṣan'ā', the capital, the rise and downfall of al-Aswad and the consequences of this; the small Muslim army found little resistance in conquering Yemen. The prophet himself had set the pattern for dealing with the Yemenis—playing one group against the other. This line of policy had some success during the prophet's lifetime, but the ripe fruits of it were picked by Abū Bakr. By contriving to rally all the opponents of Qays b. Makshūḥ, the by then shaky ruler of Ṣan'ā', around the Muslim commander who had arrived in Yemen with recruits from friendly tribes along his way—the first caliph of Islam succeeded in bringing all Yemen under Muslim control. The Yemeni tribes had been immigrating northwards for a long time before Islam; and the Muslim expansion movement supplied them with an outlet for their inclination to seek settlement in other lands. Therefore, the tribes of Yemen were among the first to join the Muslim army which invaded Syria.

In north-eastern Arabia, on the Persian border, the situation among the Arab tribes called for Medinan intervention; the door was open for an invasion of the Syrian Desert by the Muslims. The situation among the tribes in that area was—in the words of M. J. Kister—as follows:

> The second half of the 6th century was a period of fundamental changes in the relations between the tribes of North-East Arabia and al-Ḥīra. The defeat of the forces of al-Ḥīra, who took part in the raids against tribes and fought in the inter-tribal encounters—undermined the prestige of the rulers in the opinion of the tribes. Privileges of guarding caravans granted to some chiefs caused jealousy and conflict between the tribes and led to clashes between them. Discontented tribes rose in rebellion against al-Ḥīra. Raids on caravans of the rulers occurred frequently and roads of commerce became unsafe; the

[9]Watt, 118.

rulers of al-Ḥīra began to lose control of the commercial roads and their prestige dwindled. The weakness of the rulers of al-Ḥīra was apparent; troops of the Persian garrison who took part in some battles on the side of loyal tribes were defeated."[10]

Hostilities between the Arab tribes in northeastern Arabia and the Persians started a long time before the Muslim invasion of that area. The first phase of these hostilities took the form of challenge to the authority of the kings of al-Ḥīrah, who were in the service of the Persians. The tribe of Yarbū', from Tamīm, fought and defeated the forces of al-Ḥīrah on the Day of Dhāt Kahf. They forced the king of al-Ḥīrah to restore to their chief his previous position as vicegerent to the king.[11] Attacks on the royal caravans by the tribes and revengeful punitive reactions by the Persians followed.[12] Refusal by the tribes to pay the tax (*itāwah*) caused the kings of al-Ḥīrah to send repressive campaigns against the tribes.[13] In all such cases, during the first phase of worsening relations between the tribes and the Persians or their agents in al-Ḥīrah, the latter enjoyed the full support of the imperial master.

The second phase of strained relations between the Arabs and the Persians began when the king of al-Ḥīrah lent his hand to the rebellious tribes against his masters. This stage ended with the murder of al-Nu'mān, last Lakhmid king of al-Ḥīrah, by the Persians, and with their entrusting another tribe with the "kingship" in that buffer state.[14] Whatever other reasons there might have been for exterminating the

[10]M. J. Kister, "Mecca and Tamīm," *JESHO*, VIII, Pt. II (Nov. 1965), 113-114.

[11]*Naqā'id Jarīr wa-ai-Farazdaq*, ed. A. A. Bevan, Ledien, 1905-1912, Vol. 1, 66.

[12]'Abīd b. al-Abras and 'Amir b. al-Ṭufayl, *Dīwān* (ed. Sir Charles Lyall), *E. J. W. Gibb Mem.*, XXI, 1913, 117-118.

[13]al-Mubarrad, II, 83.

[14]Lewis, 33.

Lakhmid dynasty,[15] it is evident that the imposition of new taxes by the Persians was a major factor causing the turmoil among the Arab tribes, and that the Lakhmids were caught in its straits. In the context of a message from the deposed Persian king Parvīz to his son Shīrūyeh, who had overthrown him—al-Dīnawarī, in his *al-Akhbār al-Tiwāl*, quotes the following passage in which Parvīz justifies his murdering al-Nu'mān: "As for what you accuse me of—killing al-Nu'mān b. al-Mundhir and passing kingship from Al 'Amr b. 'Adīy to Iyāz b. Qabīṣah—this was because al-Nu'mān and his family made a common cause with the Arabs and told them to anticipate that sovereignty would pass from us [*Persians*] to them [Arabs]. Letters by him to this effect fell into my hands; so, I killed him and appointed in his stead another Arab who is unconscious of all that."[16]

As for the question: what cause had al-Nu'mān taken up in common with the Arab tribes?—the sources supply only meager information. Ibn 'Abd Rabbihi, in a section of his *al-'Iqd al-Farīd*, speaks of a delegation of tribal chiefs sent by al-Nu'mān to the Persian court. Kister claims that the story is apocryphal.[17] He might be right, as far as the speeches included in the story are concerned. Those speeches are given as samples of eloquent oratory, and it might very well have been a later forgery by a later author who composed them with the idea of what should have been said on such an occasion. But it is doubtful that the whole story is an invention. As in all the narratives of *Ayyam al-'Arab* (the battle days of the Arabs), a grain of truth around which a story is woven exists; which seems to be the case with this story.

According to the narrative of *al-'Iqd*, al-Nu'mān visited the Persian court while delegations from Byzantium, India, and China were there. Al-Nu'mān boasted of Arab glory and the

[15]Cf. Kister, *op. cit.*, 114-115.

[16]Abū Hanīfah Aḥmad Ibn Dāwūd al-Dinawarī, *al-Akhbār al-Tiwāl*, 109-119.

[17]Kister, *op. cit.*, 114.

Persian king scorned him and disdained the Arabs. Nu'mān defended the Arabs eloquently, and the king was astounded by his eloquence. Among other things that al-Nu'mān said in praise of the Arabs was that they refused to pay a tax under oppression.[18] When al-Nu'mān returned to al-Ḥīrah, the story continues, he invited several chiefs from the tribes of Tamīm, Bakr b. Wā'il, 'Amir b. Ṣa'ṣa'ah, Sulaym, Zubayd, and Murrah. When those chiefs had arrived at his palace, al-Khawarnaq, he addressed them saying: "You have known these A'ājim ['dumb Persians'], and how close to their borders Arabs live. And I have heard things from Kisrā [a Persian king] which I suspect have far-reaching import. Otherwise he might have brought them up with the intention of making the Arabs servile to him, like others of his servants, by imposing a tax [Kharāj] on them, the way he behaves with the kings of neighboring nations."[19] It is the tax that seems to be at the core of the whole issue.

Furthermore, beneath the rhetoric of the speeches in this story, there is a common general theme, which is the Arab refusal to pay a tax; and although it is not always stated overtly, allusions are made to it. The underlying tone of the speeches is threat—threatening Kisrā with revolt if he presses the matter too far, and what is meant by "matter" is the tax. Especial vehemence is expressed in the speech attributed to Ḥājib b. Zurārah, a Tamīmī chief, whereby an open threat is hurled at Kisrā.[20] No less violent was the speech of the renowned poet-warrior 'Amir b. al-Ṭufayl, chief of 'Amir b. Ṣa'ṣa'ah.[21] In an exchange of recriminations between Kisrā and the chief of Shaybān, the former accuses the latter of breaking an agreement concluded between the two concerning payments of land rent.[22] This episode (of the arrival

[18]Ibn 'Abd Rabbihi, *'Iqd*, II, 7-9.
[19]*Ibid.*, 10.
[20]*Ibid.*, 12.
[21]*Ibid.*, 18.
[22]*Ibid.*, 17.

of Arab chiefs in a delegation to the Persian court) taken against the background of the foregoing description of the situation among the tribes on the borders of the empire, indicates an attempt by Persia to tighten its grip on the tribes and to tax them. It is evidence, as well, of growing bitterness among the tribes, bitterness which reached a degree of defiance toward the master's authority auguring the third phase of worsening relations between the two.

The third phase of the conflict was opened by tribes attacking imperial troops and raiding imperial territory. These attacks were in retaliation for the extermination of the Lakhmid dynasty by the Persian king and were conducted by tribes who remained loyal to that royal Arab family. This phase paved the way for successful Muslim invasion of Iraq. With regard to this phase, al-Dīnawarī quotes the following report:

> They said: when Būrān [daughter of Kisra b. Hurmuz] became queen, news that there is no king in Persia and that the Persians seek refuge at the doorsteps of a woman spread through the whole world. Two men from the tribe of Bakr b. Wā'il rose in rebellion; one of them was called al-Muthannā b. Ḥārithah al-Shaybanī, and the other Suwayd b. Quṭbah al-'Ijlī. They, with their forces, proceeded and encamped on the borders of the Persian territory, and they began to raid the Persian landlords [dahāqīn] and to plunder whatever they could. Whenever pursued, the raiders retreat deep into the desert and nobody follows them up. Al-Muthannā used to raid the area of al-Ḥīrah and Suwayd that of al-Ubullah [a place near Baṣrah]. That happened during the caliphate of Abū Bakr. Al-Muthannā, therefore, wrote to Abū Bakr, informed him about his voracity in the land of the Persians and drew the caliph's attention to the Persian's weakness. Al-Muthannā asked Abū Bakr to reinforce him with an army.

Abū Bakr dispatched Khālid b. al-Walīd to Iraq.[23] Shaybān, the tribe of al-Muthannā, was the one that dealt the Persians an embarassing defeat on the Day of Dhū Qār.[24] This proposal that the caliph of Islam join in with the tribes on the Persian border in raiding imperial territory opened the gates wide for Muslim invasion of that area, and, eventually, secured its success.[25] Those tribes who were facing an eventual severe punishment for their unruly disposition and misconduct towards their master found in the Muslims a badly needed ally. For the Muslims, on the other hand, the proposal for an alliance was too good an opportunity to let slip through their fingers, and so Khālid immediately set out to put it to work.

The situation among the Arab tribes on the Byzantine border resembled, to a large degree, that among those on the Persian side. But while no contact had been made during the prophet's lifetime with the tribes on the Persian side, Muḥammad paved the way for Abū Bakr's success among the Arabs on the Byzantine side. Once and again, it has been emphasized above that the prophet and his successor championed a policy of expansion towards Syria. But it is mainly due to local factors in Syria itself that Abū Bakr's policy met with success on this front. As Goubert put it, "Maurice, by tearing the Ghassanid Kingdom; Phocas, by starting the war with the Persians, and Heracleus, by stopping the stipend to the Arabs, had created the suitable climate for the Arab invasion."[26] Following the destruction of the Ghassanid Kingdom, in the early eighties of the sixth century, the Arab tribes then under its aegis split into little groups, each under its own chief.[27] Furthermore, these splinters were maltreated by Heracleus,

[23]al-Dinawarī, 111-112.

[24]Carl Brockelmann, 8; Wellhausen, *Skizzen*, VI, 37-38.

[25]Cf. also, Lewis, 53; Kister, 115-116.

[26]P. Goubert, "Le problème Ghassanide à la veille d'Islam," *Congrès des Etudes Byzantines*, I, Act. VI (1950), 118.

[27]Theodor Nöldeke, *Die Ghassanischen Fūrsten* (Arabic tr. by P. Jousé and C. Zurayk, Beirut, 1933), 33.

and this caused them to make common cause with the Muslims.[28] In addition to this, the Byzantine army in Syria had for a long time been a sort of police force, but lacking in training as a consequence of negligence and political calculations by the Byzantines themselves.[29] Combined, all these factors greatly facilitated the Arab conquest of Syria.

In conclusion, the first caliph of Islam—by adopting a daring activist policy of expansion, while being supported by a determined group of Muslims unified by a new and fresh ideology and motivated by highly promising material gains—exploited to the utmost the favorable circumstances in neighboring areas and secured success.

[28] *Ibid.*, 49; also, De Goeje, 29; H. Lammens, "Fatḥ al-'Arab Sūrīyah wa-al-jaysh al-Bizanṭi," *al-Mashriq*, 30, 338-39.

[29] Goubert, *op. cit.*, 117.

BIBLIOGRAPHY

SOURCES

'Abīd b. al-Abras and 'Amir b. al-Ṭufayl, Dīwān, ed. Sir Charles Lyall, E. J. W. Gibb Mem., XXI, 1913.

Abū 'Ubayd al-Qāsim ibn Sallām, (770-837), *Kitāb al-amwāl*, Cairo, 1934.

Abū Yūsuf, al-Kūfī, Ya'qūb ibn Ibrāhīm, (731-798), *Kitāb al-Kharāj*, Cairo, 1933.

al-'Aynī, Maḥmūd ibn Aḥmad, (1360-1451), *'Umdat al-qārī sharḥ Ṣaḥīḥ al-Bukhārī*, 25 Vols., Cairo, 1929.

al-Baghawī, al-Ḥusayn ibn Mas'ūd, (d. 1117 or 1122), *Ma'ālim al-tanzīl* (in the margin of *Tafsīr al-Khāzin*), 7 Vols., Cairo, 1961.

al-Baghdādī, 'Abd al-Qādir ibn 'Umar, (1621-1682), *Khizānat al-adab wa-lubb lubāb lisān al-'Arab*, 2 Vols., Cairo, 1929.

al-Baghdādī, 'Abd al-Qāhir ibn Ṭāhir, (d. 1037), *al-Farq bayn al-firaq*, ed. Muḥammad 'Abd al-Ḥamīd, Cairo, 1959.

al-Balādhurī, Aḥmad ibn Yaḥyā ibn Jābir, (d. 892), *Ansāb al-ashraf*, Vol. I, ed. Muḥammad Ḥamidullah, Cairo, 1959.

————, *Futūḥ al-buldān*, ed. Ṣalāḥ al-Din al-Munajjid, 3 Vols., Cairo, 1956-1960.

al-Bayhaqī, Aḥmad ibn al-Ḥusayn, (994-1066), *al-Sunan al-kubrā*, 10 Vols., Hayderabad, 1925-1937.

al-Dhahabī, Muḥammad ibn Aḥmad, (1274-1348), *al-'Ibar fī khabar man ghabar*, 4 Vols., al-Kuwayt, 1960.

————, *Siyar a'lām al-nubalā'*, 3 Vols., Cairo, 195-.

————, *Tārīkh al-Islām*, 6 Vols., 1948(?).

al-Dīnawarī, Abū Ḥanīfah Aḥmad ibn Dāwūd, (d. 895), *al-Akhbār al-ṭiwāl* ed. 'Abd al-Mun'im 'Amir, Cairo, 1960.

al-Diyārbakrī, Ḥusayn ibn Muḥammad ibn al-Ḥasan, (16th century), *Tārīkh al-khāmīs fī aḥwāl anfas nafīs*, 2 Vols., Cairo, 1866.

al-Ḥalabi, 'Alī ibn Ibrāhim, (1567-1635), *Insān al-'Uyūn* (known as *al-sīrah al-Halabīyah*), 3 Vols., Cairo, 1964.

Ḥassān ibn Thābit, (d. 674), *Sharḥ Diwān Hassān ibn Thābit al-Ansārī*, ed. 'Abd al-Raḥmān al-Barqūqī, Cairo, 1963.

al-Haythamī, Nūr al-Dīn 'Alī ibn Abī Bakr, (1334-1405), *Majma' al-zawā'id wa-manba' al-fawā'id*, 10 Vols., Cairo, 1933-34.

Ibn 'Abd al-Barr, Yūsuf ibn 'Abdullah, (978-1071), *al-Istī'āb fī ma'rifat al-aṣḥāb*, 4 Vols., ed. 'Alī Muḥammad al-Bajjāwī, Cairo, 1960.

Ibn 'Abd Rabbih, Shihāb al-Dīn Aḥmad, al-Andalusī, (860-940), *Kitāb al-'iqd al-farīd*, ed. Aḥmad Amīn, Aḥmad al-Zayn, Ibrāhīm al-Abyārī, 3 Vols., Cairo, 1940-42.

Ibn Abī al-Ḥadīd, 'Abd al-Ḥamīd ibn Hibat Allāh, (d. 1257 or 1258), *Sharḥ nahj al-balaghah*, ed. Muḥammad Abū al-Faḍl Ibrāhīm, 20 Vols., Cairo, 1959-64.

Ibn 'Asākir, 'Alī ibn al-Ḥasan, (1106-1176), *Tārīkh madīnat Dimashq*, ed. Ṣalāḥ al-Dīn al-Munajjid, Damascus, 1951——.

Ibn al-Athīr, 'Izz al-Dīn, (1160-1233), *al-Kāmil fī al-tārīkh*, 12 Vols., (photocopy of the Tornberg edition), Beirut, 1965.

Ibn Ḥabīb, Muḥammad, (d. 860), *al-Muḥabbar*, ed. Ilse Lichtenstädter, Hyderabad, 1942.

Ibn Ḥajar, al-'Asqalānī, Aḥmad ibn 'Alī, (1372-1449), *al-Iṣābah bi tamyīz al-ṣaḥābah*, 4 Vols., Cairo, 1939.

Ibn Ḥanbal, Aḥmad ibn Muḥammad, (780-855), *al-Musnad*, ed. Aḥmad Muḥammad Shākir, 15 Vols., Cairo, 1949-50.

Ibn Isḥāq, Muḥammad, (d. 768), ('Abd al-Malik ibn Hishām, d. 834), *Sīrat al-nabī*, ed. Muḥammad 'Abd al-Ḥamīd, 4 Vols., Cairo, 1963.

Ibn Kathīr, Ismā'īl ibn 'Umar, (1301 ca.-1373), *al-Bidāyāh wa-al-nihāyah fī al-Tārīkh*, 14 Vols., Cairo, 1932-1939.

Ibn Qutaybah, 'Abdullah ibn Muslim, al-Dīnawarī, (828-889?), *Kitāb al-imāmah wa-al-siyāsah*, ed. Muḥammad Maḥmūd al-Rāfi'ī, Cairo, 1957.

————, *al-Ma'ārif*, ed. Tharwat 'Ukkāshah, Cairo, 1960.

Ibn Sa'd, Muḥammad, (d. 845), *Biographen Muhammeds*. . .(known as *al-Tabaqāt al-kubrā*), ed. Edward Sachau, Leiden, 1904-1940.

Ibn Sayyid al-Nās, Muḥammad ibn Muḥammad, (1263-1334), *'Uyūn al-athar fī funūm al-maghāzī wa-al-siyar*, 2 Vols., Cairo, 1937.

al-Iṣbahānī, Abū al-Faraj, 'Alī ibn Ḥusayn, (897?-967), *Kitāb al-aghānī*, 25 Vols., Beirut, 195-/1964.

al-Jāḥiz, 'Amr ibn Baḥr, (d. 869), *al-'Uthmānīyah*, ed. 'Abd al-Salām Muḥammad Hārūn, Cairo, 1955.

al-Maqrīzī, Aḥmad ibn 'Alī, (1364-1442), *Kitāb al-nizā' wa-al-takhāṣum fī mā bayn banī Umayyah wa-banī Hāshim*, Cairo, 1937.

al-Mas'ūdī, 'Alī ibn Ḥusayn, (d. 956?), *Kitāb al-tanbīh wa-al-ishrāf*, Cairo, 1938.

al-Mubarrad, Abū al-'Abbās Muḥammad ibn Yazīd, (826-898), *al-Kāmil*, ed. Muḥammad Abū al-Faḍl Ibrāhīm and al-Sayyid Shiḥātah, 4 Vols., Cairo, 1956.

al-Mufaḍḍal al-Dabbī, (d. ca. 784), *al-Mufaḍḍalīyāt*, ed. C. Lyall, Oxford, 1918-1921.

Naqā'iḍ Jarīr wa-al-Farazdaq, ed. A. A. Bevan, Leiden, 1905-12.

al-Nawbakhtī, Abū Muḥammad al-Ḥasan ibn Mūsā, (d. before 922), *Firaq al-Shī'ah*, al-Najaf, 1959.

al-Nuwayrī, Aḥmad ibn 'Abd al-Wahhāb, (d. 1332), *Nihāyat al-arab fī funūn al-adab*, 18 Vols., Cairo, 1923-55.

al-Rāzī, Fakhr al-Dīn Muḥammad ibn 'Umar, (1149- or-50/1210), *al-Tafsīr al-kabīr*, 32 Vols. (Vol. VIII, *Mukhtaṣar al-Muzanī*), Cairo, 1961.

al-Shaybānī, Muḥammad ibn al-Ḥasan, (ca. 750-804), *Kitāb al-siyar al-kabīr*, com. by al-Sarakhsī, ed. Muḥammad Abū Zahrah and Muṣṭafā Zayd, Cairo, 1958.

al-Suhaylī, 'Abd al-Raḥmān ibn 'Abd Allāh ibn Aḥmad, (1114-1184), *al-rawḍ al-unuf*, Cairo.

al-Ṭabarī, Muḥammad ibn Jarīr, (838-923), *Annales*, 15 Vols., (known as *Tārīkh al-rusul wa-al-mulūk*), ed. M. J. de Goeje, Leiden, 1879-1901.

al-Wāqidī, Muḥammad ibn 'Umar, (747-823), *Kitāb al-Maghāzī*, 3 Vols., ed. Marsden Jones, Oxford, 1966.

Wathīmah ibn Mūsā ibn al-Furāt, Abū Yazīd, al-Fārisī, al-Faṣawī, (d. 851), *Wathīma's Kitāb ar-Ridda aus ibn Hagar's Iṣāba*, Akademie des Wissenschaften und der Literatur, Abhandlungen, 1951, no. 4, by Wilhelm Hoenerback, Meinz, 1951.

Yaḥyā ibn Adam, (d. 818), *Kitāb al-kharāj*, Cairo, 1929.

al-Ya'qūbī, Aḥmad ibn Abī Yaqūb, (d. 897), *Tārīkh al-Ya'qubī*, 2 Vols., Beirut, 1960.

STUDIES

ARABIC

al-'Alī, Ṣāliḥ Aḥmad, *Muḥāḍarāt fī tārīkh al-'Arab*, Baghdad, 1964.

————, *al-Tanẓīmāt al-ijtimā'īyah wa-al-iqtiṣādīyah fī al-Baṣrah fī al-qarn al-awwal al-hijrī*, Baghdad, 1953.

al-Dūrī, 'Abd al-'Azīz, *Baḥth fī nash'at 'ilm al-tārīkh 'ind al-'Arab*, Beirut, 1960.

———, *Muqaddimah fī tārīkh ṣadr al-Islām*, Beirut, 1961.

Fayṣal, Shukrī, *Harakāt al-fatḥ al-Islāmī fī al-qarn al-awwal*, Cairo, 1956.

Ḥamidullah, Muḥammad, *Majmū'at al-wathā'iq al-siyāsīyah lil-'ahd al-nabawī wa-al-khilāfah al-rāshidah*, Cairo, 1956.

Haykal, Muḥammad Ḥusayn, *Hayāt Muḥammad*, Cairo, 1963.

Horovitz, Josef, *al-Maghāzī al-ūlā wa-mu'allifūhā*, tr. by Ḥusayn Naṣṣār Cairo, 1949.

Ḥusayn, Ṭāha, *al-Fitnah al-kubrā*, Cairo, 1961.

Kaḥḥālah, 'Umar Riḍā, *Mu'jam qabā'il al-'Arab*, Damascus, 1949.

al-Khuḍarī, Muḥammad, *Itmām al-wafā' fī sīrat al-khulafā'*, Cairo, 1960.

———, *Muḥāḍarāt tārīkh al-umam al-Islāmīyah*, 2 Vols., Cairo, 1956.

———, *Nūr al-yaqīn fī sīrat sayyid al-mursalīn*, Cairo, 1963.

Lammens, Henri, "Fatḥ al-'Arab sūrīyah wa-al-jaysh al-Bizantī," *al-Mashriq*, 30, pp. 337-346.

Mājid, 'Abd al-Mun'im, *al-Tārīkh al-siyāsī li-al-dawlah al-'Arabīyah*, 2 Vols., Cairo, 1956-57.

Nöldeke, Theodor, *Umarā' Banī Ghassān*, (his *Die Ghassanischen Fürsten* Arabic tr. by Pendali Jousé and Costi Zurayk), Beirut, 1933.

Wellhausen, Julius, *Tārīkh al-dawlah al-'Arabīyah*, (his *Das arabische Reich und sein sturz*, tr. into Arabic by Muḥammad 'Abd al-Hādī Abū Rīdah), Cairo, 1958.

EUROPEAN

'Arafāt, Walīd, "An interpretation of the different accounts of the visit of the Tamīm delegation to the Prophet in A.H. 9," *B.S.O.A.S.*, 17 (1955), pp. 416-425.

Becker, Carl H. "The expansion of the Saracens," *The Cambridge Medieval History*, Vol. II, New York, 1913.

Blachère, Régis, *Le problème de Mahomet*, Paris, 1952.

Bousquet, G. H., "Observations sur la nature et les causes de la conquête arabe," *Studia Islamica*, 6, (1956), pp. 37-52.

———, "Quelques remarques critiques et sociologiques sur la conquête arabe et les théories émises à ce sujet," *Stud. Orientalist. Levi della Vida*, I, (1956), pp. 52-60.

Brockelmann, Carl, *History of the Islamic Peoples*, tr. J. Carmichael and M. Perlmann, New York, 1960.

Caetani, Leone, *Annali dell Islam*, 10 Vols., Milano, 1905-26.

————, *Chronographia Islamica*, Paris, 1912.

————, *Studi di Storia Orientale*, Vol. 3, Milano, 1911-14.

Canard, Marius, "L'Expansion Arabe: Le problème militaire," *L'Occident et l'Islam Nell'Alto Medioevo*, (centro Italiano di Studi Sull'Alto Medioevo, Settimane di Studi Dell...XII), Spoleto, 1965, Vol. I, pp. 37-63.

Eickelman, Dale, "Musaylima," *Journal of the Economic and Social History of the Orient* (JESHO) X, pp. 17-52.

Gaudefroy-Demombynes, Maurice, *Mahomet*, Paris, 1957.

Gibb, Sir Hamilton Alexander Rosskeen, *Studies on the Civilization of Islam*, Boston, 1962.

Goeje, Michael Jan de, *Mémoir sur la conquête de la Syrie*, Leiden, 1900.

Goubert, P., "Le problème Ghassanid à la veille d'Islam," *Congrès des Etudes Byzantines*, Vol. I, Act VI, 1950, pp. 103-118.

Hamidullah, Muḥammad, "Les Ahābīsh' de la Mecque," *Stud. Orientalist. Levi della Vida*, I, (1956), pp. 434-447.

————, *Corpus des traités et lettres diplomatiques de l'Islam ā l'époque du prophète et des kalifes orthodox*, Paris, 1935.

————, *Documents sur la diplomatie Musulmane à l'époque du prophète et des kalifes orthodox*, Paris, 1936.

————, "Al-īlāf, ou les rapports economico-diplomatiques de la Mecque pré-islamique," *Mélange L. Massignon*, II, (1957), pp. 293-311.

————, *Le prophète de l'Islam*, 2 Vols., Paris, 1959.

Hitti, Philip Khuri, *History of the Arabs*, 6th Ed., New York, 1956.

Hottinger, Arnold, *The Arabs*, University of California Press, 1963.

Hurgronje, C. Snouck, *Selected Works*, tr. and ed. by J. Schacht and Bousquet, Leiden, 1957.

Kawar, Irgan, "The Arabs in the peace treaty of A.D. 561," *Arabica* 3, (1957), pp. 181-213.

Kister, M. J., "Mecca and Tamīm , aspects of their relation," *Journal of Economic and Social History of the Orient*, Vol., VIII, Part II, 1965, pp. 113-63.

Lammens, Henri, "Le triumvirat: Aboū Bakr, 'Omar, et Aboū 'Obeida," *Mélanges Université Saint-Joseph* (MUSJ), 4, (1910), pp. 113-144.

Laoust, Henri, *Les Schismes dans l'Islam*, Paris, 1965.

Lewis, Bernard, *The Arabs in History*, London, 1958.

————, ed., *Historians of the Middle East* (with Holt), London, 1962.

Muir, Sir William, *The Caliphate, Its Rise, Decline, and Fall*, (new edition revised by T. H. Weir), Edinburgh, 1924.

———, *The Life of Mohammed*, (a new edition revised by T. H. Weir), 2 Vols., Edinburgh, 1912.

Pareja, F.M., *Islamologia*, Orbis Catholicus, Roma, 1951.

Rosenthal, Franz, *A History of Muslim Historiography*, Leiden, 1952.

Sauvaget, J., *Introduction to the History of the Muslim East*, Los Angeles, 1965.

Tyan, Emil, *Institutions du Droit Public Musulman*, Paris, 1954.

Watt, W. Montgomery, *Muḥammad at Medina*, Oxford, 1956.

Wellhausen, Julius, *Skizzen und Vorarbeiten*, 6 Vols., Berlin, 1884-1899.

INDEX

www.ingramcontent.com/pod-product-compliance
Ingram Content Group UK Ltd.
Pitfield, Milton Keynes, MK11 3LW, UK
UKHW041911310325
456954UK00003B/82

9 781487 580995